W9-CDS-708

WITHDRAWN

WITHDRAWN

GROWTH AND STRUCTURE OF
DISTANCE EDUCATION

GROWTH AND STRUCTURE OF DISTANCE EDUCATION

BÖRJE HOLMBERG

CROOM HELM
London • Sydney • Wolfeboro, New Hampshire

© 1986 Börje Holmberg
Croom Helm Ltd, Provident House, Burrell Row,
Beckenham, Kent, BR3 1AT
Croom Helm Australia Pty Ltd, Suite 4, 6th Floor,
64-76 Kippax Street, Surry Hills, NSW 2010, Australia

British Library Cataloguing in Publication Data
Holmberg, Börje
    Growth and structure of distance education.
    1. Distance education
    I. Title
    371.3   LC5800
    ISBN 0-7099-4748-8

Croom Helm, 27 South Main Street,
Wolfeboro, New Hampshire 03894-2069, USA

Library of Congress Cataloging-in-Publication Data

Holmberg, Börje.
    Growth and structure of distance education.

    Bibliography: p.
    Includes index.
    1. Distance education. 2. Distance education—
Philosophy. 3. Distance education — History. I. Title.
LC5800.H64 1986   378'.03   86-16744 ·
ISBN 0-7099-4748-8

Printed and bound in Great Britain
by Billing & Sons Limited, Worcester.

378.03
H747g

CONTENTS

44049

CONTENTS

CONTENTS

PREFACE

Evolution, continuity and development are the themes
of this book. The rationale, principles and
practice of distance education since its inception
as an organised activity are looked into. A number
of issues are shown to have been concomitants of the
applications of distance education throughout its
history.

While concentrating on the problems and ideas
behind distance education the book pays considerable
attention to modern practice. Some parts of the
presentation of methodology represent brief
references to or abbreviated expositions of concerns
more fully discussed in the author´s book on the
state of the art.(1)

I am indebted to Mr.M.K. Newell, Vice Chairman
of Wolsey Hall, Oxford, and Mr. D.R. Kazmierski,
Vice President, Educational Services, National
Education Corporation, Scranton/PA, for placing
early documents of importance at my disposal.

Börje Holmberg

(1) Holmberg, B. (1985), Status and trends of
    distance education, second revised edition,
    Lector Publishing, Box 14010, S-22014 Lund,
    Sweden.

PLUS ÇA CHANGE, PLUS C'EST LA MÊME CHOSE.

Chapter 1

THE CONCEPT OF DISTANCE EDUCATION

Distance education is a term that has only gradually become accepted. A kind of formal recognition occurred in 1982 when the International Council for Correspondence Education (ICCE) changed its name into the International Council for Distance Education (ICDE) (ICDE minutes 1982, p.30). This change of name illuminates the fact that the basic origin of distance education is correspondence education, known and practised since at least the latter part of the 19th century. In fact, there are indications that the terms distance education, distance study and distance teaching, although apparently not originating in German usage, at an early stage often occurred as translations of German words like Fernstudium, Fernlehre and Fernunterricht, traditional designations for correspondence education in Germany (Holmberg 1974, p.1, Peters 1969 p.94). It is interesting to note that the Council of Europe symposium on the role of correspondence tuition within multi-media learning systems at Bad Godesberg and Berlin as early as September 1972 used distance education as synonymous with modern correspondence education. (1)

Correspondence study has gradually developed in a way to include a number of media apart from printed texts and interaction in writing, for instance recordings of the spoken word, radio and TV, video recordings, telephone and computer communication, and for this reason many educators, particularly in the UK, prefer retaining the term correspondence education to distance education. However, as most people seem to regard correspondence as something that takes place entirely in writing, distance education has been adopted as a more neutral term. It can be considered a wider, inclusive designation. The same

1

has been claimed about the term independent study in North America.(2) Interestingly enough this designation occurs in an English prospectus as early as 1914, but in the sense of study ´with no examination in view` (Wolsey Hall 1914 p.20).

Distance education thus includes the various forms of study at all levels which are not under the continuous, immediate supervision of tutors present with their students in lecture rooms or on the same premises, but which, nevertheless, benefit from the planning, guidance and tuition of a tutorial organisation. This definition of mine (Holmberg 1977a p.9) has been widely accepted (cf. Keegan 1980a and b, whose propositions have been analysed by Bååth 1981). Distance study denotes the activity of the students, distance teaching that of the tutorial organisation, particularly its authors and tutors. The main characteristic is non-contiguous communication.

Distance education comprises one-way traffic by means of printed, broadcast and/or recorded presentations of learning matter and two-way traffic between students and their supporting organisation. The one-way presentation of learning matter occurs either through self-contained courses or through study guides to prescribed or recommended reading. Most of the two-way traffic usually occurs in writing, on the telephone or by other media and, usually only secondarily and as a supplement, face to face.

An interpretation that insists on mediated two-way communication as a <u>sine qua non</u> would exclude most of the present-day activities in the Socialist countries in Europe that are described there as distance education (<u>Fernstudium</u> in the GDR) as these for the element of real communication do not - or merely to a small extent - rely on mediated two-way traffic; they replace it by face-to-face sessions (Möhle 1979). Something similar applies to the Dutch Open Universiteit. In a paper entitled ´Pride and prejudice among distance educators` Bååth discusses the dilemma and suggests a very wide distance-education concept. He argues that

> ...distance study programmes vary from almost no tutor-student two-way communica- tion at a distance to a great concern for distant communication and dialogue. They also vary from almost no concern for the teaching functions of the distant learning

material to extremely elaborated study material, intended to provide all learning support possible within the framework of the study package. This may be illustrated by means of the following categorization of different types of self-study and distance education...:

		None	Little	Great
	Great	7	8	9
TWO-WAY COMMUNICATION	Little	4	5	6
	None	1	2	3

None Little Great

Teaching functions of the learning material

Only type 1 is definitely not a kind of distance education. All the other types exist as variations of distance education (although some authors prefer to exclude types 2 and 3).

(Bååth 1984a pp.70-71)

Delling 1985a in a delineation of distance education in relation to pure self study comes to a similar conclusion. To him the realisation of communication predominantly by technical media is a characteristic of distance education; however, his wording seems to indicate that a printed or recorded course transferring learning matter to the student (one way) combined with any type of two-way communication, evidently also face to face, is taken to meet his requirements.

My definition of 1977 as quoted above would thus seem to stand also by the standards of Bååth and Delling. However, within this wide description we can identify two extreme interpretations (and applications), one insisting on exclusively non-contiguous, i.e. mediated, two-way communication (by correspondence or tele-interaction), the other representing face-to-face interaction on the basis of distance-teaching materials. Between these extremes there are various intermediary positions acknowledging face-to-face interaction as a subsidiary procedure, for instance on the one hand that of the British Open University which, though catering for complete non-contiguous two-way communication, systematically organises face-to-face contacts in study centres and at summer courses, on the other hand that of many private distance-teaching organisations in Europe, the USA and elsewhere, which offer two-way communication mainly by non-contiguous means, but make occasional use of face-to-face sessions.

Evidently it is in the nature of distance education that it serves the individual learner in the study he/she does on his/her own. At the same time courses developed can easily, and to great financial advantage, be used by great numbers of students, and - in fact - distance education can be - and often is - a form of mass communication. This unity of individualisation and mass communication may appear as something of a paradox. Personal approaches and a conversational style are compatible with individualisation. In preparing a mass communication programme, on the other hand, it is practical to apply the methods of industrial work. These methods include planning, rationalising procedures, division of labour, mechanising, automation, and controlling and checking. Peters has made a systematic study of these methods and has compared them with industrial work. He describes distance study as an industrial type of teaching and learning (Peters 1973 and 1983).

The technological approaches implied do not prevent personal communication of a conversational character from being the backbone of distance study. This applies even when computerised communication occurs. I regard organised distance study as a mediated form of guided didactic conversation.

Distance study is self-study, but the student is not alone; he benefits from a course and from interaction with tutors and a supporting organisation. A kind of conversation in the form of two-way traffic occurs through the written and telephone interaction between the students and tutor and others belonging to the supporting organisation. Indirectly conversation is brought about by the presentation of study matter as this one-way traffic causes students to discuss the contents with themselves. The conversation is thus both real and simulated. The simulated conversation

4

is not only what Lewis calls internalised conversation caused by the study of a text (Lewis 1975 p.69), but is a relationship between the course developers and the students created by an easily readable and reasonably colloquial style of presentation and the personal atmosphere of the course, superficially characterised by, for instance, the author(s) referring to himself/ herself/themselves as I or we respectively and the students being spoken to as you ('I recommend that you...'). Questions and replies, suggestions and references to problems known to the students belong here. This style of presentation stimulates activity and implies reasoning, discussing for and against, referring to the student's previous experience and thus avoiding omissions in chains of thought. Revision tasks and self-checking exercises also belong to the simulated conversation. The wish to avoid compactness causes a certain amount of redundancy in conversational texts.

My theory of distance study as a mediated form of guided didactic conversation will be looked into further in Chapters 5 and 8.

NOTES

1. The terms education by correspondence or 'distance education' connote systems of teaching and learning based mainly on non-personal media, whose efficiency for student performance is controlled by two-way communication (feedback). (The Council of Europe Annual Report 1972, p.5).

2. Cf. Wedemeyer, who claims that 'independent study, a term now used in the United States as generic for the several kinds of distance and non-traditional learning systems that include correspondence study', is more precise than distance education. 'The term, in addition, has significance respecting learning theory, and has historic continuity, at least in the United States'. (Wedemeyer 1981, p.50).

Chapter 2

PIONEERING WORK IN DISTANCE EDUCATION

Whereas the term distance education is a fairly
recent adoption, the concept it covers as described
in Chapter 1 is at least 150 years old. Teaching by
correspondence in a non-organised fashion is, of
course, much older, as witnessed for instance by the
Biblical epistles meant for the instruction of early
Christian congregations. Gerhard Terstegen, Mme de
Sévigné and others have been referred to in this
context (Delling 1964 and 1978, H. Graff 1964), and
in the context of distance education correspondence
related to social distance belonged to the first
themes theoretically analysed (K. Graff 1964).

When organised distance education first
occurred is not undisputedly clear. The earliest
mention so far known of what could be distance
education has been found in ´The Boston Gazette` of
20 March, 1728,in which ´Caleb Philipps, Teacher of
the New Method of Short Hand` advertises that any
´Persons in the Country desirous to Learn this Art,
may by having the several Lessons sent Weekly to
them, be as perfectly instructed as those that live
in Boston` (Battenberg 1971 p.44). Some doubt
whether this information really concerns distance
education inclusive of two-way communication between
learner and teacher has been expressed; it may
simply refer to self-instructional material, a
category of publications well known in the 18th and
19th centuries (Bååth 1980 p.13 and 1985 p.61). If
this is the case it seems remarkable that the
lessons should be sent weekly. Probably a week was
regarded as a suitable period for the solution of an
assignment given; it is possible either that such
solutions were submitted to the teacher or that the
students themselves corrected them, using model
answers or comments provided for the purpose. We
seem at least to be entitled to give Caleb Philipps´

6

claim (by proxy) to be a pioneer in the field of distance education the benefit of the doubt.

About a hundred years later we find more conclusive evidence of distance education in our sense. An advertisement in English in ´Lunds Weckoblad`, No. 30, 1833, a weekly published in the old Swedish university city of Lund, offers ´Ladies and Gentlemen` an opportunity to study ´Composition through the medium of the Post` (Bratt 1977 p.161; also referred to, after Bratt, in Bååth 1980 p.13 and Bååth 1985 p.62). Another early attempt to organise distance education was made in England by Isaac Pitman who reduced the main principles of his shorthand system to fit into postcards. He sent these to students, who were invited to transcribe into shorthand short passages of the Bible and send the transcription to him for correction. This teaching of shorthand combined with a study of the Scriptures began in the year 1840 when in the United Kingdom the uniform penny postage was introduced. In 1843 the Phonographic Correspondence Society was formed to take over these corrections of shorthand exercises. It was the beginning of what was later to become Sir Isaac Pitman Correspondence Colleges (Dinsdale 1953 p.573, Light 1956, The Times of 24 December, 1952).

According to early tradition, organised distance education is assumed to have been introduced in Germany in the year 1856 by the Frenchman Charles Toussaint and the German Gustav Langenscheidt, who formed and organised a school in Berlin for language teaching by correspondence (Noffsinger 1926 p.4). What scope the correspondence actually had is uncertain; students were offered opportunities to submit questions, but, Bååth writes, translating from the Toussaint-Langenscheidt prospectus, ´they were by no means encouraged to do so - "it would hardly be necessary", the prospectus said, "since everything is fully explained in the course"` (Methode Toussaint-Langenscheidt, 1901?, p.10)(Bååth 1975 p.62; cf. also Delling 1978 and Sommer 1965).

A pioneer of some interest is mentioned by Mathieson as a representative of the ´proto-correspondence study programs` that existed in the United States between 1865 and 1890:

> The "mother" of American correspondence study was Anna Eliot Ticknor, daughter of a Harvard University professor, who founded and ran the Boston-based Society

to Encourage Study at Home from 1873 until her death in 1897. The idea of exchanging letters between teacher and student originated with her and monthly correspondence with guided readings and frequent tests formed a vital part of the organization´s personalized instruction. Although the curriculum reflected the "classical orientation", it is interesting that most of her students were women, a clientele then only beginning to demand access to higher education.

(Mathieson 1971 p.1)

A most important early distance-teaching activity originally based on the development and distribution of self-instructional material was the so-called ´Methode Rustin` known from 1899 (Delling 1985a p.9). The Rustin approach is interesting as it is consistently based on a plan developed as a general guideline for correspondence courses, on which further in Chapter 3.

Among British pioneering organisations were Skerry´s College, Edinburgh, founded in 1878 (preparing candidates for Civil Service Examinations), Foulks Lynch Correspondence Tuition Service, London, 1884 (specialising in accountancy), University Correspondence College, Cambridge, founded in 1887 and preparing students for University of London external degrees (in 1965 this college was taken over by the National Extension College [Perraton 1978 p.1]), and the Diploma Correspondence College, now called Wolsey Hall, Oxford,(1) founded in 1894, preparing students for university qualifications but also offering a wide range of courses on other subjects (Dinsdale 1953).

In the latter half of the nineteenth century the university extension movement in England and the U.S.A. promoted the use of the correspondence method. Among American pioneers in this context should be mentioned Illinois Wesleyan College, 1874, the Correspondence University (Ithaca, N.Y.), 1883, and the University Extension Department of Chicago University, 1890 (Mathieson 1971 p.3). This is an American testimony from 1900:

Correspondence between leaders of thought and their followers has always played an important part in the development of knowledge. The constant allusion to

correspondents in Darwin´s Autobiography affords an illustration in point. The formal and systematic methods of correspondence teaching have, however, been developed only within the past two decades. In 1880 work of this sort was being carried on by a society in Edinburgh. At the same time Dr. William R. Harper, in this country was offering instruction in Hebrew by mail. In 1881 the Chautauqua Correspondence College made its definite announcements, and began systematically a work which, for a year or two, had been done in a less formal fashion....
    In 1892 the University of Chicago began its work, and at the outset correspondence instruction was an organic part of the teaching methods of the institution. Since that time, the University of Wisconsin and the University of West Virginia have made provision for the same sort of teaching.

(George E. Vincent 1900)

A less academic American origin is found in an attempt to teach mining and methods of preventing mine accidents which was introduced by a course in 1891 constituting a systematised continuation of an instructional activity begun earlier in a question column in the Mining Herald, a daily newspaper published in the coal mining district of eastern Pennsylvania. The initiator of the correspondence course was the editor of this newspaper, Thomas J. Foster. His initiative met with great success, and the response his course won led to the production of first an extended course of the same type and then to the preparation of a number of correspondence courses in various fields. In fact, this was the beginning of the International Correspondence Schools (ICS) in Scranton, Pennsylvania, and their subsidiaries and offshoots (Correspondence Instruction 1901). Their historical connection with Scranton and Pennsylvania is made explicit in an early document:

The origin and location in Scranton, Pa., of the Schools are due to the demand by the miners of Pennsylvania for special education to help them pass the mine-law examinations.

(General Circular 1900, p.4)

9

Later developments show that the provision of both academic and practical occupational study opportunities was to be typical of distance education in the 20th century. Another pioneer illustrating this is Hermods in Sweden, founded in 1898 and later to become one of the world´s largest and most influential distance-teaching organisations (see Chapter 3). It is interesting to note that H.S. Hermod, the founder of Hermods, started his distance-teaching activities as a result of an idea about how to help an individual student and allegedly without any influence from American correspondence education (Gaddén 1973 pp. 39-41). Hermod had been in charge of a language school in Malmö since 1886 and had there applied what he called the Nature Method in teaching English by means of self-instructional lessons (which were printed also in a periodical). This was a method taken over from the German ´Methode Haeusser`, on which see Chapter 3. A student who had to leave Malmö, but was anxious to continue his English course, was then taught by correspondence. ´The student received long letters in English and answered them in English to the best of his ability` (Carne 1957 p.44). This proved a satisfactory and successful arrangement and caused Hermod to develop assignments based on the self-instructional courses. In 1898 and 1899 he then advertised his offer of correspondence courses in double-entry accountancy etc. He had made a similar attempt in 1892 by means of some duplicated course units in English - at that time without success. According to what he said himself in 1918 he had then learnt from the German Langenscheidt courses how to avoid the mistakes made in his first attempt (Korrespondens 1918 p.293, quoted in Gaddén 1973 p.40).

Since the time of the First World War distance education has been introduced in country after country so that now it is known all over the world. Among the pioneering activities should be mentioned at least two initiatives from the first four decades of this century. They concern distance education in Australia, USA and France.

Australia is today a country and a continent with its own systems of distance education at the tertiary level, which date back as far as 1911 when the Universiy of Queensland entered the field of distance education (Store & Chick 1984 p.57). They are influential and internationally important as will be seen in the following discussion in Chapter 4 and elsewhere. Another Australian pioneering activity concerns primary and secondary education, however. It has gradually developed into a sophisticated, highly successful type of activity (cf. Taylor & Tomlinson 1985 and Tomlinson, Coulter & Peacock 1985). It belongs to the type of distance education that is usually called supervised correspondence study. This term denotes the study of correspondence courses under the guidance of a teacher who need not - and cannot - be academically competent in all the subjects learnt but who advises and supports his pupils and is a link between the supporting organisation and the learners (Childs 1963, Holmberg 1973). It has been said that:

> Australia can claim to be the first country to have shown in a systematic way, and on a large scale, that it was possible to provide by correspondence a complete primary and secondary education for children who had never been to school.

(Rayner 1949 p.12)

The author quoted continues:

> Victoria and New South Wales were first in the field of primary correspondence work. Both helped other States to initiate similar schemes, which each State has varied to suit its own particular needs...
> Correspondence courses at the secondary level have developed from two sources: the need to educate teachers, and the desire of some who had finished the primary course to continue their studies. In the early years of this century many pupils who had completed their primary courses joined the Education Departments as pupil-teachers. They taught by day and continued their education at night to complete the academic courses that were a pre-requisite to promotion. To help young people stationed in isolated rural areas some States provided courses to matriculation level. The Victorian scheme, begun in 1910, was the first. In several States

secondary tuition by correspondence was reserved for teachers, but the higher educational standard required of entrants to the teaching profession has lessened this need and, with the demand of the armed services for correspondence tuition during the war years, the courses were thrown open to all.

During the late twenties and early thirties the worth of the existing primary courses was apparent; pupils who had completed the primary course had expressed a desire for further education and there were also pupils in the upper grades of the smallest rural schools ready to use post-primary courses. The secondary courses were developed and extended until now, in any State, it is possible for a pupil to receive a complete secondary education by correspondence.

(Rayner 1949 pp.12-13)

It is interesting to note that this Australian supervised correspondence education began as a result of an individual initiative, which recalls the beginning of Hermods in Sweden in 1898:

In May 1914, the Victorian Education Department received a letter from a settler in Beech Forest, living eight miles from the nearest school. In this letter he enquired, "Can anything be done for the education of my two boys?" The Chief Inspector referred the request to Mr. J. McRae, Vice-Principal of the Teachers´ College, in the hope that he might be able to arrange for some of the students in training to send lessons by post. As a result, five students volunteered to try the plan of teaching the boys by correspondence. Each one undertook responsibility for certain subjects. Sets of work for each fortnight were prepared and regularly posted. The children were instructed in the ordinary subjects of the curriculum, including the making of systematic observations of weather phenomena and of plant and animal life. At the end of the year the boys attended the nearest school and sat

successfully for the annual school examination. In the following year their instruction was continued in the same way,
and a younger brother of five was added to
the class.

(Rayner 1949 p.15)

An American presentation of 1934 referred to
these Australian experiences and added:

The movement spread to the other provinces
of Australia, to New Zealand, to West
Africa, and to Canada. Today these
countries educate thousands of isolated
children by this method. Correspondence
courses were first used to enrich the
secondary school curriculum in the United
States in 1923, at Benton Harbor,
Michigan. There S.C. Mitchell, realizing
that the average high school program does
not begin to meet the needs and desires of
the great majority of students, began to
experiment with supervised correspondence
courses. His high school of seven hundred
students was offering a variety of
academic courses, but provided few courses
of a vocational nature compared with the
range of students' interests and needs.
Mr. Mitchell then turned to the nearest
Correspondence Center offering vocational
courses, The American School, and then
also to the International Correspondence
Schools, and made special arrangements for
use of courses from these two
Correspondence Centers. Last year,
1933-1934, this program had expanded until
one hundred thirty-two students were
enrolled in correspondence courses in
Benton Harbor, with a variety of over four
hundred different types of courses from
which to choose....
      In 1928, the Sixth Yearbook of the
Department of Superintendence on the
Development of the High School Curriculum
suggested the use of supervised
correspondence courses. In 1929 the
University of Nebraska began experiment-
ation with the use of correspondence
courses in high schools. In 1931, upon
receiving a grant from the Carnegie

Foundation for the Advancement of Teaching, a department was set up within the Extension Division of the University which is devoted exclusively to the preparation and administration of such courses.

(Report of supervised correspondence study 1934 pp.8-9)

The French pioneering work mentioned had a somewhat different start as described by Hilary Perraton

In France, in 1939, the government realized that the education of school children would be at risk as teachers were called up and children evacuated. With Gallic logic they decided that if the schools were not to stay open, alternatives would have to be found, and the Ministry of Education set up a government correspondence college, now the Centre National de Télé-Enseignement. It did its immediate job of providing an alternative education for school children. More important in the long run, its proven value in 1945 meant that the Centre was continued as a regular part of the state educational system.

(Perraton 1978 p.2)

It is only fair to mention that this centre, now called Centre National d´Eseignement par Correspondance, after the war has become a huge distance-teaching organisation which mainly caters for adult education and is only marginally concerned with supervised correspondence education for children and adolescents.

With the various pioneering developments indicated by the examples referred to distance education had been firmly established. It would seem to be worth while looking further into early distance education before a study of present-day application is embarked on.

NOTES

1.   The school was originally based in
Bristol. When the founder ´moved from Bristol to
Oxford in about 1906 he picked up the name Wolsey
Hall from the building in which he moved. The
building itself picked up the name from one of the
co-founders of the Oxford College who owned it,
namely Christchurch College founded initially by
Cardinal Wolsey` (private communication of 1 March,
1985, from Mr. M.K. Newell, Vice Chairman of Wolsey
Hall and grandson of the founder).

Chapter 3

THE RATIONALE AND BASIC CHARACTERISTICS OF EARLY DISTANCE EDUCATION

Adults with occupational, social and family commitments were the original target group of distance education - and this is the one still mainly catered for. These students wish to educate themselves in their spare time either to improve and update their professional knowledge or to widen their intellectual horizons generally, to learn for practical purposes, for instance applications of computer technology or a foreign language, or to acquire knowledge and insight for its own sake. To the generations that were young when the first correspondence schools and similar distance-teaching organisations started their work, the opportunities they offered were very often the only chances available to compensate for faulty or insufficient early education. Distance education gave - and gives - gifted and hard-working people a possibility to study beside their jobs and other commitments. In some countries it had and may still have a pronounced careerist character. It served and serves upward mobility educationally, professionally and socially. The following seems to be typical of early approaches to distance education.

> Our correspondence teaching meets an important need. It affords anyone an opportunity to educate himself/herself further; it gives to young men and women anxious to make progress an opportunity to reach an independent position and to poor people a possibility to work themselves free of their poverty. The student can learn without neglecting his daily work, make use of his leisure time and in this way acquire valuable, practical knowledge. Each student constitutes his own school

16

class. He can choose what time suits him
for his study and can at will use any hour
available to learn.

(Translation from the Hermods prospectus
of 1908 p.10)

Similar arguments can be found in prospectuses
published elsewhere in the world. They have
something to say about the target groups of the
early organisations and also about their educational
aspirations. Individual learning and flexibility as
to time and place of study is regularly stressed
along the lines indicated by Hermod in the above
quotation and in the following sentence: ´Anyone
can...begin at any time...and is guaranteed tuition
until he has finished his course` (ibid., p.12).
Individualised teaching (Hermod, ibid., p.12,
stresses that a correspondence tutor works with one
student at a time only and sometimes the personal
relation between students and tutors (Hermod 1908,
p.11) are frequently referred to. These
characteristics can be subsumed under the concepts
customer orientation or student friendliness, which
will be looked into further in Chapter 7. So can
attempts to apply what has later been called ´the
spiral curriculum` (Ausubel 1968, p.209). This
procedure, well known in modern distance education
(cf. Holmberg 1985a pp.54-55), was consistently
applied in the German ´System Karnack-Hachfeld` in
1896 (van den Berg 1984, p.105). Student autonomy
is also related to ´student friendliness`. It is a
concept that sometimes merely seems to imply
independence in absorbing prescribed texts and in
other cases includes independent critical
approaches, problem solving, judgment of proposed
solutions and more. This is one of many early
statements bearing on this:

Self-confidence is engendered. The student
is taught to exert his faculties to the
utmost and to rely upon himself without
receiving too much help before he performs
his task.

(Wolsey Hall Prospectus 1914, p.9)

The procedures applied have varied considerably
from the very beginning, which is not surprising
considering the occurrence of distance education in
different countries and contexts independently of

one another. Here some early examples:

William Harper, USA

This is how William Harper, the first President of the University of Chicago and in America often referred to as the father of correspondence teaching, described the work:

A brief explanation of the plan of study by correspondence is first in order.

1. An instruction sheet is mailed to the student each week. This instruction sheet (a) assigns the tasks which are to be performed, e.g., the chapters of the text to be translated, the sections in the grammar to be learned; (b) indicates an order of work which the student is required to follow; (c) offers suggestions on points in the lesson which are liable to be misunderstood; (d) furnishes special assistance wherever such assistance is deemed necessary; (e) marks out a specified amount of review work; (f) contains an examination paper which the student, after having prepared the lesson, is required to write out. The instruction sheet is intended, therefore, to guide and help the student just as an oral teacher would guide and help him.

2. The examination paper is so constructed that, in order to its preparation for criticism [sic], one must have prepared beforehand most thoroughly the lesson on which it is based. An examination paper on Caesar, for example, requires of the student (a) the translation of certain chapters into English; (b) the translation into Latin of a list of English sentences based on the Latin which has just been translated; (c) the explanation of the more important constructions, with the grammatical reference for each construction; (d) the placing of forms; (e) the change to "direct discourse" of a corresponding passage in "indirect discourse"; (f) the explanation of geographical and historical allusions; (g) the statement of grammatical principles, etc., etc.

3. In the <u>recitation paper</u> submitted to the instructor, besides writing out the matter called for in the <u>examination paper</u>, the student asks such questions, and notes such difficulties, as may have presented themselves to him in his study of the lesson. This recitation paper is promptly returned with all errors corrected, and questions answered; and with special suggestions, suited to each individual case.

In this manner each lesson of the course is assigned and studied; and the results of the study submitted to the instructor for correction, criticism, and suggestion.

From this it will be seen that the correspondence teacher must be painstaking, patient, sympathetic, and <u>alive</u>; and that the correspondence pupil must be earnest, ambitious, appreciative and likewise <u>alive</u>. Whatever a <u>dead</u> teacher may accomplish in the classroom, he can do nothing by correspondence; and if a student lacking the qualities just named undertake work by correspondence, one of two things will happen: either he will acquire these qualities, and succeed; or he will remain as he was at the beginning, and fail. The man who does the work at all, must do it well.

(From John H. Vincent [ed.] 1886 pp. 183-193, quoted from Mackenzie & Christensen 1971, pp.8-9)

ICS, USA

The ´method of instruction` applied by the International Correspondence Schools (ICS) from the beginning is described as follows:

As soon as the student is enrolled, his first and second Instruction and Question Papers are sent to him, accompanied by directions for proceeding with the work, "Information Blanks", and a supply of envelopes.
After carefully reading the directions, he studies the first

Instruction paper, and works out the examples for practice. If he meets with any difficulty, he fills out an Information Blank, giving full particulars, sends it to the Schools, and proceeds with his studies. A full written explanation of the matter is promptly forwarded from the Schools, and he is encouraged to write for special information at any time. After mastering the contents of the first Instruction Paper, he takes up the accompanying Question Paper, and writes his answers to the test questions. He then forwards these answers to the Schools, and proceeds to study the second Instruction Paper.

When the sets of answers are received at the Schools they are first reviewed by women examiners specially trained for this work. They carefully go over the work, checking in red ink such errors as exist in arithmetic, spelling, punctuation, etc. The answers are then submitted to the Principals and male Instructors for final examination and correction of such subjects as the examiners are not competent to correct. When an error is discovered, it is not only indicated in red ink, but a careful explanation of that particular problem is written on the back of the sheet. Whenever necessary, special exercises and letters of explanation are sent to the student.

After being corrected, the Papers are entered upon the books as passed if a mark of 90 per cent has been attained; which is generally the case if the student has carefully studied the Instruction Paper. If his mark falls below 90 per cent, he is required to review the incorrect portions until mastered. The answers are then returned, accompanied by a Percentage Slip and the third set of Papers. By this system the student always has one Paper to study while his work in a previous Paper is being corrected.

(General Circular 1900, p.6)

Apart from the startling reverence shown to male staff members this ICS method became very influential in distance education generally.

Hermods, Sweden

A comparison with Hermods in Sweden may be a worthwhile study. In the first number of 'Korrespondens', published in 1901, Hermod gives a rather full presentation of the method he applied. The teaching material was provided in the form of printed course units, 'letters', of 4, 8, 12 or 16 pages to which were usually added 'special question letters', i.e. assignments for submission.

As soon as a student has enrolled he receives two teaching and question letters as well as detailed instructions how to use the letters. After he has studied the first teaching letter he puts it aside and starts work on his question letter, answering each question in the order in which it occurs. Then he puts his work into an envelope provided with our address and sends it by mail. When these answers have arrived at the Institute they are scrutinised very carefully there and, when all mistakes have been corrected in red ink, the answers are returned together with such comments and explanations as will make it possible for the students fully to understand the subject. Every mistake is marked and everything is explained completely. Experience shows that these written comments are more easily remembered than oral comments. After the student has submitted his answers to the first question letter he starts studying teaching letter No. 2 following the same procedure as he applied when studying the first letter. When the corrected replies to question letter No. 1 are returned, it is accompanied by teaching letter No. 3 and question letter No. 3. When he receives letters No. 3 the student puts them aside until he has finished No. 2; not until the replies to No. 2 have been sent (to the Institute) does he begin with No. 3 etc. In this way he has always a letter ready at hand to study while the earlier one is being corrected. If after careful study of some topic a student does not fully understand

21

it he has only to send in a question about
the difficulty. As soon as such a
question has been received it is answered
immediately.

(Korrespondens 1, pp.13-14) (1)

In the second issue of ´Korrespondens`, also
published in 1901, Hermod compares correspondence
teaching with oral teaching. Among other things he
writes:

One student may complete a course in three
months and another the same course in two
years, but both in any case attain their
goal. This cannot be said about oral
teaching as in this case the individual
student must keep the same pace as his
fellow students or be left behind.
    In correspondence education there are
no vacation times. Nothing interferes
with or interrupts the students´ work.
People can begin their studies on any day
of the year they prefer and can be equally
sure to get careful teaching at whatever
time they begin. Studies can be
interrupted whenever the student wishes to
do so and be taken up again when it suits
him.

(Korrespondens 2, p.29)

Rustin, Germany

The German Rustin courses followed a detailed
guideline representing the ´Methode Rustin`, which
was practised from 1903 (Delling 1966, p.19). Every
course unit is developed in the following way:

1. Subject matter presentation in a self-
   instructional form.
2. Conversation about the subject matter,
   in which the main points of the
   subject matter presentation are
   repeated by questions and answers.
3. A summary.
4. Revising questions with references to
   the sections of the subject-matter
   presentation where the answers to the
   questions are to be found.
5. Exercises in the form of questions

developed in such a way that the students must be able to answer them on the basis of what has been learnt through the preceeding parts of the course unit. The correct answers to these questions are provided at the beginning of the following course unit.

6. Individual correspondence teaching aimed at developing autonomous thinking by means of a comprehensive assignment to be performed in writing.

(Delling 1966, pp.19-20)

This method has exerted considerable influence on German distance teaching, both in the Federal Republic and in the GDR (Delling 1966).

The conversational approach is striking also in the early Hermods courses. The adaptation of the German ´Methode Haeusser` which characterised the early language courses of Hermods - like the original Haeusser claims to represent a school of conversation in which every sentence occurring in the foreign-language texts is treated dialogically (Gaddén 1973, pp.27-33).

Wolsey Hall, England

Whereas Hermods insisted on entirely self-contained courses, others applied the study-guide approach. This is how distance learning was described at an early stage by Wolsey Hall:

Method of work

Text-Books - The Tutors take special pains to select, in each subject or branch, the book or books which they consider most suitable for the Examination contemplated or for the particular purpose in view. The subject matter of the book is divided up into a number of Lessons of about equal length, the last two or three being of a Revision nature.

Books may be borrowed from the College Lending Library, or may be bought on easy instalment terms (see p.12). If the student desires a Course in any particular book this can be arranged.

<u>Schemes of Study</u>, stating the titles, publisher and price, of the necessary text-books and of books useful for supplementary reading, and showing the arrangement of the Lessons in each subject and in each branch of the subject, are sent to the student on receipt of his Entry Form.

<u>An Enrolment Form</u> accompanies the schemes of Study, containing:
  (a) A list of all the Lessons the Student is to receive.
  (b) Dates on which the various Lessons are to be sent.
  (c) Names and addresses of the Tutors to whom his work is to be sent for correction.
  (d) Regulations and full instructions as to method of procedure.
  (e) The Guarantee (p.10) signed by the Principal.

<u>Separate Lessons</u> are sent not only in each subject, but in each branch of the examination, that they may have them always at hand for reference and revision.

<u>Time of Starting</u>. - As the tuition is <u>entirely individual</u>, students can be admitted <u>at any time</u>. To derive, however. the greatest benefit from the Course, Candidates should take as long as possible over it. The work may be spread over any period without increase of fee. As the same number of Lessons is sent in every case, it is clear that the earlier a student starts work for any examination the fewer the number of Lessons to get done each week, and consequently the longer the time that can be devoted to each.

<u>Holidays</u>. - The work of the College goes on all the year round. Students, however, who join long enough before their examination, and who desire holidays either for recuperation or or for revision of back work, may have their Courses arranged to admit of holidays whenever

they wish, provided full instructions are given to the Registrar on joining the College.

Postponement of Examination.- Students falling behind with their work may have their Course re-arranged either for the same or for a later Examination on payment of a re-distribution fee of 2s. 6d. In cases where there is a change of Syllabus, special authors, etc., a proportionate charge will be made for any special Lessons already sent that are not required for the new Exam.

Privacy. - All communications are treated as strictly private, plain envelopes are used, and names of successful students are not advertised without their consent.

x)   See note p.10, on meaning of "week". (2)

(Wolsey Hall 1914, pp.6-7)

William Lighty, USA

One of the great American pioneers, William Lighty of the University of Wisconsin, in 1915 identified essential characteristics, requirements and potentials of distance education. The following extracts will illustrate this:

In extramural teaching must be created the method, the technique, the atmosphere which shall give the university a new meaning in democracy. For him (= the 'extramural teacher') it is to solve the difficult problems connected with long distance instruction. Their solution has hardly begun. He must be able to do more than correct errors and communicate information. He must put into his instruction his personality, his inspiration, his interpretation, as the painter puts his on the canvas, or as the musician puts his into his composition. So far as his pupils bring to the instruction the capacity of appreciating what is communicated, so far will they benefit just as in the case of the canvas

25

or the musical composition. The supreme test of teaching is the capacity to do this, and in no fields is there so fine an opportunity as exists in extramural teaching. In an assemblage like this the possibility of doing this will not be questioned, for we know it is daily done. Some extramural teachers go so far as to use two colors of ink on the recitation papers: one for correction of errors and the like, and another color for the comments of instruction and interpretation in which they communicate themselves. Thus, the teacher-pupil relation in correspondence-study becomes very real, very personal, and indeed very intimate...

The new type of teacher and the new type of text and instruction are required because we have a new type of student from that in the conventional school. He is generally an adult student. He has a fairly definite idea as to what he needs and wants, and often an almost equally definite idea as to what he does not want. He has to be convinced by logic and experience, and not by rule of order, of the position of the teacher, for none of the ordinary compulsions operating in the intramural instruction are effective here. The student makes up his mind quite promptly on an early, if not the first, examination of the lessons or course as to whether it is worth his while...

With the type of student suggested, it follows that there must be changed standards of success and failure for extramural students. A man may go through half or a third of a course and get all he needs or wants to satisfy his original purpose. It would be folly to apply conventional pedagogue standards, which tend automatically to class him as a failure. Likewise, many other factors that surround the study conditions of the extramural student require adjusted standards of success and failure.

Extramural teaching in the university answers to the social present-day demand for a share in the intellectual and spiritual pleasures and the material

benefits of the accumulated knowledge and
wisdom of the race. This is the demand
for the opportunity to know - educational
rights. This, I take it, is quite akin to
the demands made earlier in social
evolution for the opportunity to vote -
political rights - or the privilege to
believe - religious rights.

(From the ´Proceedings of the first con-
ference` [National University Extension]
as reprinted in Mackenzie & Christensen
1971, pp.19-21)

Similarities and differences

Basic arguments in favour of distance education
voiced from the very beginning are thus the
opportunities opened to adults to learn anywhere and
at any time suitable to them beside their other
commitments, to upgrade their competence and
generally to educate themselves without having to
adapt themselves to the convenience of others.
Learning was often encouraged as a way for the
leisure-time student to better himself/herself and
to climb professionally, socially and financially.
Methodologically individualisation, flexibil-
lity, student friendliness and student autonomy were
considered characteristics worth aiming at and were
apparently partly attained. There is a difference
here between on the one hand Hermod´s and Lighty´s
full liberalism, on the other hand approaches
including more control; cf. Harper´s rule that an
´instruction sheet is mailed to the student each
week` which may reflect a type of pacing well known
in universities offering distance study, but
contrary to the Hermod-Lighty approach. It is
interesting to note that Wolsey Hall, while catering
for free pacing (´Lessons may be taken weekly,
fortnightly or monthly, or even daily or half-weekly
to suit the student´s conveniences`), insisted that
what is called worked exercises ´should be
dispatched by the student on the day that his next
batch of lessons is sent, i.e. on Friday to reach
his Tutor on Saturday.`... ´Regularity and
punctuality are insisted upon as they are a great
stimulus to steady work` (cf. extract on pp.23-25).
As evident from what has been said, some of the
earliest arguments in favour of distance education
are still relevant. They are quoted again and again.
Thus in 1901 H.S. Hermod wrote: ´In correspondence

education each student constitutes his own class and form` (Korrespondens 1901, p.14) and Wolsey Hall made it clear that `the tuition is entirely individual; students can be admitted at any time` (Wolsey Hall 1914, p.7). These arguments have retained their importance. In 1985 Hermod´s latter-day compatriots in the distance-teaching school of the Swedish Telegraph and Telephone Corporation which provides computerised courses, made use of a cartoon with the following question and answer: `What class are you in? - I am in a class of my own` (Från vision 90 till verklighet, 1985, p.10).

NOTES

    1.   Translated - like other passages from Swedish and German sources - by the author.
    2.   The note referred to runs like this: `The word "week" is used in a technical sense, and means the period of time arranged to elapse between the receipt of one Lesson and the next` (ibidem p.10).

Chapter 4

THE BEGINNING OF A NEW ERA OF DISTANCE EDUCATION -
INNOVATORY EVOLUTION RATHER THAN REVOLUTION

From the beginnings described in Chapters 2 and 3 a
steady expansion of distance education occurred
until around 1970 without any general radical change
in organisational structure, but with gradually more
sophisticated use of methods and media, for example
audio recordings in language teaching and in courses
for blind people and the use of laboratory kits in
subjects like electronics, radio engineering etc.
The founding of the British Open University in 1971
marks the beginning of a new era, in which degree-
giving distance-teaching universities with full
degree programmes, sophisticated courses, new media
and systematic systems evaluation crop up in various
parts of the world and confer prestige on distance
education. See Rumble & Harry 1982.

Whereas up to the 1960s the large-scale
distance-teaching organisations had - with very few
exceptions - been private correspondence schools
(one of which - Hermods in Sweden - had since 1959
been an official examining body for its own
students), the new era saw publicly supported and
established universities and schools becoming more
and more important. An outstanding pioneer in this
respect is the University of South Africa, which
emerged as a development of the University of Good
Hope, founded in 1873 as an examining body based on
the model of the University of London. It started
teaching at a distance in 1946. The University of
South Africa was definitely established as a
distance-teaching university through a governmental
decree of 1962 (Boucher, 1973).

What above all gives us reason to regard the
early 1970s as the beginning of a new era in
distance education is the new public recognition
since then usually given to this kind of education.
With few exceptions, as in Scandinavia, educational

29

authorities had until then been sceptical in their appraisal of correspondence study. The founding of publicly funded universities basing their work on distance-education methods changed this. The creation of the Open University in the United Kingdom can be seen as the beginning of a more prestigious era in the history of distance education. The image changed in several countries from one of possibly estimable but often little respected endeavour to one of a publicly acknowledged type of education far from seldom acclaimed as an innovative promise for the future.

The new distance-teaching universities

At the outset there was much belief in radio and above all TV as the teaching medium in the new public distance-teaching universities. In the UK the original plans for the Open University referred to it as ´The University of the Air`; this is the title of a Government White Paper of February 1961 outlining ´plans for drawing on new technological advance to establish an "open university" to cater for the thousands of potential students who are unable to enter the conventional universities` (Home Study 1, p.5). When the FernUniversität (= the Distance University) had been founded in Hagen in West Germany the Prime Minister of Northrhine-Westphalia in his opening speech on 4 October 1975, again and again made the Freudian mistake to call it the ´Fernsehuniversität` (= the TV University). The new distance-teaching universities very soon made the printed and written word their main media, however.

The reasons for founding the distance-teaching universities were mainly

o   the need felt in many countries to increase the offer of university education generally

o   a realisation that adult people with jobs, family and social commitments constituted a large group of prospective part-time university students

o   a wish to serve both individuals and society by offering study opportunities to adults, among them disadvantaged groups

o   the need found in many professions for

    further training at an advanced level

o   a wish to support educational innovation

o   a belief in the feasibility of an economical use of educational resources by mediated teaching.

Inherent in these reasons is the wish to cater for permanent or recurrent education, for social equality, expressly and frequently mentioned in the early debate (cf. Burgess 1972 and Woolfe 1974) and sometimes expressed as a wish to attract ´working-class students` (Woolfe 1974, p.41; McIntosh, Calder & Swift 1976, p.VIII, 98-106, and elsewhere).

The objectives listed above occur in different forms in documents paving the way for the distance-teaching universities; also special training needs are sometimes referred to. Information about these universities has been collected in Kaye & Rumble 1981, which lists the following founded in the 1970s:

> Allama Iqbal Open University, Pakistan
> Athabasca University, Alberta, Canada
> Everyman´s University, Israel
> FernUniversität, West Germany
> Free University of Iran
> Open University, UK
> Sri Lanka Institute of Distance Education
> Universidad Estatal a Distancia, Costa Rica
> Universidad Nacional Abierta, Venezuela
> Universidad Nacional de Educacion a Distancia, Spain

To these could be added similar organisations like:

> Open Learning Institute, British Columbia, founded in 1978
> Open Universiteit, The Netherlands, starting in 1984
> Kyongi Open University, Korea (1982)
> Korea Correspondence University, South Korea (1972)
> Universitas Terbuka, Indonesia (1984)
> Sukhothai Thammathirat Open University, Thailand (1978)
> Sri Lanka Open University, Sri Lanka (1981)
> Central Broadcasting and Television University, China (1978)

University of the Air, Japan (1983)
The Open School, India (1980)
Indira Gandhi National Open University, India
(1985)

These organisations have already become important
and have, in fact, largely succeeded in meeting
their objectives. They also exert general influence
on the methodology and the use of media in distance
education.

The correspondence schools

In the 1950s and 1960s the large-scale
correspondence schools had undergone successive but
considerable changes. Much attention had been given
to new developments (systems approach, media etc.).
The ICCE conference in Paris in 1969 (Erdos 1969)
and the work done in the American and European
professional organisations bear witness to this (the
Home Study Review 1960-1967, published by the US
National Home Study Council, the CEC Yearbooks from
1965, the journal Epistolodidaktika published by the
Hamburger Fernlehr-Institut in the 1960s and by the
European Home Study Council from 1971, as well as
numerous conference and workshop reports). In their
further development they represent sophisticated
types of distance education which from the points of
view of didactics characterise the new era in a way
comparable to that of the new distance-teaching
universities.

Distance education in university departments

Decentralised distance-teaching facilities
offered by traditional universities, either building
on earlier work as in Australia and North America
(Dahllöf 1976, Smith 1979 and 1984, Wedemeyer 1981,
Ashworth 1978 and 1979, Vonk & Brown 1978 etc.) or
new as in the 1970s in Sweden and the Argentine, for
example, represent other facets of the new era. The
Australian University of New England is particularly
interesting as the extreme opposite of the large-
scale systems represented both by the distance-
teaching universities and many correspondence
schools.
In principle in the New-England system a
university lecturer engaged both in on-campus and
distance teaching develops a distance-study course
for his/her own group of students; he or she
personally undertakes the tutoring, both at a

distance and face-to-face. Far-reaching parallelism
with on-campus study (tutors, examinations etc. in
common) is aimed at and attained in the professed
interest of academic standards and credibility.
This New-England practice has been taken over by
most universities and colleges in Australia and also
by some elsewhere, for instance in Zambia (Sheath
1969, p.131).

A new Australian university beginning teaching
at a distance in the late 1970s but with a modified
approach is Deakin University in Victoria, like the
University of New England a 'dual-mode' institution,
i.e. one with both on-campus and off-campus
students. Deakin is highly innovatory, developing
inter-disciplinary courses, paying much attention to
instructional design, turning mature students'
independence to account and thus applying liberal
approaches, requiring no compulsory attendance at
face-to-face sessions etc. (cf. Castro & Holt 1985).

The innovatory character of modern distance
education

The developments that led to what I have called
a new era of distance education are firmly based in
the traditions as described in Chapters 1-3. This
is evident when the innovatory character of distance
education is looked into. If innovation is in this
context seen as far-reaching use of the potentials
of distance education, then the innovatory character
of this kind of education is derived from:

o   the underlying ideas that learning can
     occur without the presence of a teacher
     and that the support given to students can
     be adapted to their standards of knowledge
     rather than to expected entrance
     qualifications;

o   the consistent use of non-contiguous media
     both for the presentation of learning
     matter and for ensuing communication;

o   the methods applied to exploit the non-
     contiguous teaching/learning situation so
     as to attain the highest possible
     effectiveness for the individual learner:
     structure and style of presentation and
     communication (didactic conversation),
     appropriate use of media available,
     adaptation to students' conditions of

life, etc.;

o   the particular organisation which makes it
possible to provide for both independent
individual learning and mass education
through personal tutoring and more or less
´industrialised` working methods;

o   the influence distance education exerts on
adult education, further training and
labour-market conditions, by opening new
study opportunities as well as through its
methods and organisation.

Innovation in formal education

Formal education has often been felt to be in
need of innovation, and it is also in study for
degrees and examinations for formal recognition that
distance education has contributed - and can further
contribute - particularly tangible innovations.

The fact that, as a rule, distant students
study only in their spare time and study on their
own, make certain suitable arrangements necessary.
There would seem to be four requirements or
desiderata congruent with the circumstances of
distance study when applied in the context of formal
education:

o   non-contiguous feedback to meet the need
for human contact and to tell students if
and to what extent they have mastered the
elements of knowledge and/or proficiency
presented in a course unit;

o   free pacing to allow students to work
when their circumstances permit
independently of any plans of their
university or school;

o   opportunities to sit for examinations
when students are ready to do so; and

o   a credit-point organisation that allows
and encourages them gradually to acquire
competence in one subject or part of a
subject after another.

As will be shown in Chapters 6 and 7 (and elsewhere
in this book) these are no unchallenged claims,
however.

The <u>feedback</u> aspect is related to the tutoring that occurs through the non-contiguous two-way communication typical of distance study. Feedback is important not only for discussion, explanation and enrichment, but also to show the student if he or she is on the right path and if he or she can continue without reviewing or practising previous learning elements.

<u>Pacing</u> imposed on distant students creates difficult problems. Adult students usually have considerable professional, social and family commitments which make it unreasonable to expect them to give first priority to their study. Instead, they have to adapt their study to their living and working conditions. They may have to do extensive travelling on business (for instance) which precludes any study during a certain period. Similar effects can be produced by childbirth, the illness of children, etc. On the other hand, adult students may have chances to take certain periods off for concentrated study. All this is highly individual. The logical, but far from uncontested conclusion is that students should be placed in a position to pace their study as they can and want to. Making certain deadlines compulsory for submission of assignments creates difficulties which are evidently often insurmountable and lead to dropping out (Bartels & Hofmann 1978).

If <u>examination opportunities</u> are few and far between, distant students are placed in difficulties. The answer is fairly simple: to provide examination facilities two to three times per term in each subject or part of subject in which marks are to be given. This means allowing students to choose the time for their examination, which is tantamount to saying they have a right to be examined when they feel prepared for it. This is nothing very revolutionary. Such a procedure has been applied by Swedish universities since the beginning of this century. (1)

A <u>credit-point organisation</u> greatly facilitates free pacing and the free choice of examination opportunities. Such an organisation of the study implies giving credits for examinations, project work and theses as well as awarding degrees on the basis of a sufficient number of such credits attained over a period of several years. A credit-point organisation of this type allows students to concentrate on one subject or part of a subject at a time. It can contribute to depth in the study at the same time as the obligation of having to master memorised details is diminished. It also means that students are given the choice of studying for a full degree or just for the subject or parts of subjects that are particularly important to them. This opens the gate for recurrent education and will, for instance, enable engineers and bank employees to acquire degree qualifications in business administration, relevant parts of political economy or law, etc., teachers to do the same in subjects not included in their original degrees, business administrators in an engineering subject or computer technology, etc. For those who want a full degree, the study can be spread out over a number of years and months, which is an important requirement for part-time study.

When the ideas expressed are accepted, a system uniting all the characteristics referred to represents the complete realisation of the innovation that distance study constitutes for formal education. It seems worthwhile finding out to what extent the characteristics actually occur and what consequences the application of the principles have. In the following a survey based on selected examples will be attempted.

The British Open University

The Open University is an apparently highly successful innovation, completely established and stabilised. It is in a way a radical innovation introducing new study methods, a new degree structure based on credit points, a new type of organisation, new categories of academic staff and new tasks for professors and lecturers. Students can be enrolled without any formal entrance qualification, and people above normal study age who are gainfully employed and who have no intention of going in for full-time study are deliberately favoured. At the end of 1984 more than 69,000 graduates had successfully completed their BA degree studies. Nevertheless, a study of what happened at the end of the 1960s and the beginning of the 1970s shows that the whole project was under threat of being stopped. There was heavy political opposition to it in Parliament and the press. In university circles it was for a long time (and may to some extent still be) regarded with suspicion and misgivings (Perry 1976, Hawkridge 1976). Non-contiguous communication, the use of self-instructional courses and the methods of educational technology, inclusive of the use of various media, were explicitly and implicitly branded as unacademic, etc. That it succeeded in such a short time is a remarkable achievement.

The Open University has become a success story. It has also faced disaster, even abolition, remarkably often in only a few years. It has been seen as a political plaything, an educational gimmick, a technological monster and a costly frippery. Others have hailed it as Britain's best contribution to education in the second half of the twentieth century, a masterly harnessing of technology to social purposes and a powerful catalyst in higher education throughout the world.

(Hawkridge 1976)

What is this success due to? First of all the intrinsic power of the idea behind it coupled with the strong political will both of the Government during the foundation period and the spokesman of the University must be considered decisive. Second, strong and diplomatic leadership evidently played an important part. The successful recruitment of enthusiastic academics as planners, course developers, tutors and counsellors, keen on the innovatory aspects of their work and attracted to the Open University because of its special character, represent a third explanation. It might seem reasonable to attribute part of the success to the Zeitgeist and to the international tendencies favouring recurrent education and unconventional approaches, but comparisons with other systems, for example the FernUniversitat (see below), hardly support this.

The Open University would seem to apply consistent distance-study principles. However, it is not a completely uncompromising innovation. It comprises some traditional characteristics that do not facilitate the distance study of adults with professional and social commitments, but constitute compromises with conventional thinking. Thus, students cannot take up study when it suits them, but have to await the beginning of the academic year. They cannot study and submit assignments when it suits them, but are bound by a pacing system imposed on them not only by TV and radio broadcasts but also by those in authority. It is apparently

the conviction of the latter that it is good for the
students to follow the pacing prescribed.

The German FernUniversität

The FernUniversitat is a younger institution
than the Open University. It began its work in
1975, limits its teaching almost exclusively to the
German university stage which, from the start, is
academically considerably more advanced than the
´foundation courses` of the Open University. A
student who can give 20 working hours a week to his
study is expected to need eight years to attain a
full degree.

The FernUniversität applies strict formal
entrance requirements for those aiming at degrees,
but has nevertheless been successful in enrolling
large numbers of students. In 1985 it had some
28,000 students. Its drop-out rate is very high
(Bartels & Hofmann 1978). The first ten years saw
some 500 graduates who had completed the full
regular curricula for a German university diploma;
another 500 had acquired other types of academic
competences by degree examinations.

The FernUniversität applies a rigorous pacing
system allowing students to submit specified
assignments during predetermined periods only. The
course materials are distributed according to
timetables set by the various faculties and
completely unrelated to the progress or wishes of
individual students. The non-contiguous teaching
occurs through pre-produced courses, with the
exception of the study of mathematics hardly through
real two-way communication, as students´ papers are
often merely ticked off and marked, rarely really
commented on, before they are returned to the
individual students and as the turn-round time is
long.

The academic standards of the FernUniversität
are very high. It seems probable that even more is
required of its graduates than of those of the other
German universities. Its study system is - as
indicated - very rigid. It applies the same
curriculum, examination and semester system as other
universities and is, on the whole, based on the
pattern of the traditional German universities.

Whereas the FernUniversität has succeeded in
introducing systematic distance study leading to
degrees, it has a long way to go to implement the
innovation inherent in its conception:
individualised study based on effective didactic

two-way communication allowing each student a high degree of autonomy.

The FernUniversität is meant to contribute to university reform in the Federal Republic of Germany and to provide new openings for further training at the university level. The absence of a German credit-point system allowing students to gain formal recognition of individual courses and/or examinations jeopardises the latter task, however, although on this point some important contributions have been made through post-graduate programmes.

Extension departments of universities

University correspondence study was - as shown above - well known long before the founding of distance-teaching universities like the University of South Africa and the Open University of the UK. It is a sideline activity of many universities in various parts of the world. Best known are, no doubt, the contributions of universities in the USA, Canada and Australia.

The Australian University of New England has already been referred to. It is a prototype of what I should like to call the small-scale approach to distance study. Whereas most distance education has something of a mass-communication character in that courses are produced for large target groups, the New England approach envisages small groups of distance students working alongside campus students. The same tutor/student ratio for distance study as for conventional study is regarded as acceptable and recommendable. This precludes any possibility to apply the ´industrial`, rationalising methods with division of labour by which distance study is normally characterised.

This model is interesting as it represents an important a-typical application of distance study, usually combined with insistence on periods of attendance for face-to-face teaching. To some extent it is similar to some American extension correspondence study. Also, it has influenced new approaches to Swedish university distance study (Dahllöf 1976). A rather extreme application is met with in the University of Waterloo cassette teaching in Canada, where explicitly the class, not the individual, is seen as the target:

Courses start and end on fixed dates. During a course there is a fixed schedule of assignments. There is an examination

> scheduled on a fixed date at the end of
> the course. We treat each student as a
> member of a class, although that class is
> geographically distributed.

(Leslie 1979, p.245)

These applications of distance study are not very radical in their deviations from traditional study. As an innovation, the New England model and its followers rather concern changes within the system than a shift of systems. Cf. Belchem´s comments on a similar system in New Zealand, in which he says that the ´very interweaving of internal and extramural study has prohibited the emergence of a genuine extramural alternative, an education provision going beyond the conventional framework, however generously defined that may be` (Belchem 1979, p.5).

The extension activities of American universities are usually considerably more liberal in allowing students to plan their work, and explicitly favour ´independent study`. As indicated above this also applies to Deakin University in Victoria, Australia.

General education at secondary level

At secondary level, correspondence education has traditionally been able to point to a number of remarkable successes. In Sweden with a total population varying between six and eight million in the years 1932-1966 no less than 2,363 students of Hermods, the leading correspondence school, passed the tough studentexamen which opened the gates of the universities, and 3,220 took the realexamen (roughly equivalent to the English O-level GCE) in the same period (Gaddén 1973, p.278). Their standards were recognised to be high, and their success led to Hermods being made an official examining institute from 1959. Some leading Swedish scholars, authors, civil servants and politicians have acquired all or most of their formal school qualifications by correspondence. Parallel developments have occurred in the USA and various European countries. Cf. Weinstock 1975.

The study methods applied have mainly been those of traditional correspondence study: pre-produced printed courses, developed for large groups of users, didactic individual non-contiguous two-way communication in writing, limited use of audio-recordings for the learning of foreign languages, sometimes supplementary face-to-face sessions before examinations and occasionally telephone tutoring. The study thus takes place outside the publicly provided system and evidently constitutes full application of the innovation of distance education: new target groups (adults gainfully employed and housewives with extremely varying educational backgrounds); methods based on non-contiguous communication and radically deviating from classroom teaching; student independence (completely free pacing and study at any time and anywhere according to individual students´ possibilities and predilections); a credit-point system; indirect influence on the public organisation of education through new study facilities and new target groups. In terms of the attainment of the formal qualifications aimed at this educational activity has been successful. It proved the effectiveness of correspondence education long before the great public systems such as the Open University made distance study well-known.

Professional qualifications

Correspondence study leading to examinations organised by professional bodies is a most important feature in the British training system, probably dating from the turn of the century or earlier. Here belong courses preparing students for the examinations of The Institute of Chartered Secretaries and Administrators, The Institute of Chartered Accountants, and a great many other professional bodies.

While there is hardly anything similar in importance to this in other countries, much distance study leading to professional qualifications occurs in countries all over the world. The USA and Western Europe, as well as countries in Eastern Europe, provide typical examples.

The innovatory value of these activities largely equals that of distance study for general education.

Meeting the innovatory requirements

The above examples have shown how the innovatory requirements of formal distance education have been aimed at and partly satisfied in well-established practice. With my starting point I have found two systems that entirely meet the

innovatory requirements identified above. They are
the secondary-level correspondence study described
above and, at the university level, one that is
regrettably largely out of action towards the end of
the 1980s. It is an activity initiated and
organised by Hermods in Sweden, publicly financed
and under the inspection of the Chancellor of the
Swedish Universities. It began in 1952 and was
particularly important in the years 1960-1972.

Frequent non-contiguous two-way communication
for tutorial and feedback purposes, completely free
pacing, a free choice of examination periods based
on concentrated study of one subject at a time and
a credit-point organisation are characteristic of
this activity. At the beginning of the study,
students receive a small number of course units.
For each end-of-unit assignment submitted for
correction and comment students receive a new course
unit. On request further units are sent to
students, for instance if they wish to concentrate
on their study during a certain period and thus plan
to complete course units at an unexpectedly high
speed. All the requirements listed above are met.
The university study offered and administered by
Hermods has proved very successful with some 4,000
degree examinations up to 1972 (Gadden 1973, p.289).
This application of distance study for university
degrees has been unanimously recognised to be of
high academic standard and of great importance for
the further education and training of gainfully
employed adults. However, it is characterised by a
considerable drop-out rate, which is no doubt due to
its open access also to students with no intention
to pass an examination (Annual reports of the
official course inspectors; in the Central Office
of the Universities, UHÄ, Stockholm, 1953-1975).

A system applying the procedures of the Person-
alised System of Instruction (PSI) or the Keller
Plan (but not necessarily the behaviourist thinking
behind them) might also be used in distance
education entirely congruently with the innovatory
requirements discussed (Holmberg 1985a, pp.145-149).

To anyone in favour of autonomous learning a
very promising development is the introduction of
individualised degree-programme planning and
teaching-learning systems based on learning
contracts, which there will be reason to return to
in the following discussion. The Empire State
College in New York is probably the best known
exponent of contract learning which, since 1979, is
catered for also by distance-education methods

through a Center for Distance Learning at Saratoga Springs. Its activity is based on three principles, i.e.:

1. that effective learning derives from the purposes and needs important to the individual,

2. that learning occurs in varied ways and places, and

3. that styles of learning and of teaching may differ significantly from person to person and from one setting to another.

(Worth 1982)

Murdoch University in Western Australia has also developed a system for contract learning at a distance (Marshall 1985).

From the above presentation it is evident that the innovatory potentials of distance education for formal <u>and</u> informal study have been applied to different degrees and that so far little used possibilities still offer themselves to educators and educational establishments prepared to derive the maximum benefits from modern distance education.

NOTES

1. Long before subjects were divided into individual courses followed by examinations, which is a widely spread procedure at present, this was the case. Thus students could register for an examination in the whole of a subject on six different occasions during the year. If they failed on one occasion they could register for a new examination as soon as they felt ready for it. Unless examination periods of this type had been advertised in advance, students in fact had the right to be examined within a fortnight after registering as an examinee (Chapter 8 of Kungl. Maj:ts nådiga stadga angående filosofiska examina of 1 November, 1907, with modifications made up to 1946). Such a system is valuable to any university student. To distant students who study as well as have a job, it would seem to be extremely important that examination opportunities are provided when they are ready to take them.

Chapter 5

PRINCIPLES FOR PRACTICE IN MODERN DISTANCE EDUCATION

The structure of modern distance education should be looked into against the background of what has been said about mediated, non-contiguous communication as the basic characteristic of distance education, about its potentials for individualisation and student autonomy, its applicability to mass communication and the innovatory resources vested in it. This will be done under five headings.

The presentation of learning matter

Distance-teaching organisations have from the very beginning largely developed fully self-contained, printed courses meant to cover the whole of the subject area taught. It has been considered valuable in the interest of effectiveness, in relation to study time invested, that students should be guided straight to specific course goals without being distracted by approaches different from those of the pre-produced course. Thus the self-contained character of the courses and the absence of books and other study material not developed specially for the distance-education courses have often been regarded as an advantage and an argument in favour of distance education, explicitly referred to by for example H.S. Hermod as early as 1901 (Korrespondens 1901, pp.12 and 47). In agreement with this thinking a number of special principles for the presentation of learning material have been developed. They include target-group analyses, readability research, procedures for sequencing and structuring, media selection, graphical and typographical design etc. and, particularly in the 1970s under the influence of behavioural psychology, the identification and wording of specified, as far as possible behavioural, study objectives. The state of the art in these respects is discussed with ample documentation in Holmberg 1985a, pp.41-86.

When at an early stage subject-matter presentation was sometimes limited to notes bearing on standard textbooks this was mainly a consequence of small student bodies which made the development of self-contained courses impossible. When the big distance-teaching universities started they - like most correspondence schools - developed - and largely still develop - fully self-contained and highly sophisticated courses of their own, apparently adopting the early Hermod thinking. As examples can be mentioned typical courses of the British Open University and the German FernUniversität, basically in print but often provided with audio cassettes, kits, micro-computer material, etc. There can be no doubt that these courses are efficient if combined with suitable communication between students and tutors, in writing, on the telephone or by other means. On condition that the students are capable of following the exposition, doing the exercises and solving the problems set, these self-contained courses with their various components are good at leading students to the specific course goals. The course developers tend to regard each study unit as an integral part and thus as a compulsory course component which is only rarely regarded as replaceable.

Sometimes the all-embracing course structure is considered too rigid. It is felt only proper that the students should be offered a choice of what units of a course are to be regarded as relevant in each individual case. Such an approach leads to each unit or each small set of units being separate and providing a sufficient treatment of a limited, and strictly defined, part of the subject. When that is the case students can build their own curricula from units or sets of units belonging to different courses. This is what in German is called the Baukasten-Prinzip, the principle of the box of bricks.

The advantage of this principle is that each study unit or set of units can be used in different contexts, which is economical and can contribute to widening the offer of educational opportunities. Further, it makes provision for requirements to study one little part of a subject only (and possibly acquiring a certificate which, through a credit-point system, can be tantamount to securing what can be regarded as a mortgage on a degree or other formal competence).

This modular principle would seem to have another consequence of considerable importance in that it lends itself to supporting the general autonomy of the students. If each unit or set of units is provided with a kind of product declaration including statements of the objectives, the availability of sufficient numbers of units on related topics will give the individual student a possibility to select his or her own study objectives.

One important aspect of student autonomy is provided for when in this way students decide what and how to study. However, the presentation of learning matter may even then be far from pluralistic, and this applies to the tutorial activity as well if it merely supports the learning provided for by the course materials. Effective distance teaching may, even though the subject areas are chosen by the student himself/herself and the teaching is made use of at the student´s own discretion, become autocratic, at least to some extent. Distance teaching may then mean ´teacher centred education, where the media are used as substitutes for the teacher, "telling" students what they ought to know` (Ljoså 1977, p.79).

This autocratic tendency is hardly compatible either with taking advanced students´ capacity for independent study into account or with developing autonomy. Various possibilities to cope with this difficulty exist.

One is, contrary to the tradition of self-contained courses, to limit the development of course materials presenting learning matter to study guides facilitating or, if necessary, steering the study of set texts. This is useful when, as in advanced study, students must be made to see a complicated picture of a subject with conflicting theories and views, or they have to learn how to trace facts and arguments from different presentations and to study various sources critically. In such cases the study-guide approach is evidently more suitable in that the study guide causes students to read and/or listen to presentations of various kind, to compare and criticise them and to try to come to conclusions of their own.

This study-guide approach is generally practical when the learning is to include part or the whole of the content of various books, papers and other sources of knowledge. When students have inadequate library facilities or when only few selected texts are relevant, the reading initiated and facilitated by the study guide may be provided in a specially prepared reader including uncensored contributions by protagonists of competing schools of thinking. This is what the present author has tried to do in his post-graduate distance-teaching course on distance education (Holmberg 1982a). On study-guide courses see further Holmberg 1977b, Ljoså 1975 and Weltner 1977.

Making regular use of scholarly papers in periodicals is one way of keeping courses up to date and relevant in this context. Re-printing, with due permission, suitable articles for distribution among students is a procedure apparently commonly adopted by, for instance, the University of Queensland. Australian copyright laws seem favourable to distance education on this point.

An interesting but little practised form of distance education by means of the printed word is to be found in newspaper courses. Here, a series of articles in newspapers, possibly inclusive of 'letters to the editor' from course participants, constitute the course text (cf. Chamberlain 1974, Stewart 1976, Dohmen 1978 and Reichmann 1979). The communication element need not differ from normal practice in distance study.

By the methods indicated some steps have been taken on the path towards independent academic study. It is possible to go further, however, and, in fact, there is an old tradition of a kind of wholly individual distance education arranged to help external students to prepare themselves for a London University degree. London University examines and confers degrees on students who have not attended any of its classes but have prepared themselves in other ways (cf. Erdos 1967, p.8). Individual students are put into contact with a university lecturer who is a specialist of the subject to be studied. This subject specialist guides the study of books included in the degree curriculum concerned, assesses the student's written work in the course of the study and acts as an adviser and as a tutor whose help can be enlisted when needed, usually by correspondence. The National Extension in Cambridge for one has advertised this kind of service to prospective London graduates (Home Study 1, p.2 and elsewhere). In this type of study there are no specially prepared distance-education courses.

Completely individualised curricula and highly autonomous study can further be brought about by contract learning at a distance, of which - as indicated above - The Empire State College in the US is a leading representative.

> Empire State College's academic programme provides students with the flexibility of time and place of study one ordinarily associates with external studies or distance learning. However, since most of the options available to students enrolled in the College are premised on the assumption that learning is most meaningful if it begins with the student's own interests, the modes of study, the content of the degree structure and the methods used in evaluation of student work are individually designed and implemented.
>
> (Coughlan 1980, p.2)

In contract learning an agreement is made between a student and a tutor (a 'contract') about a certain curriculum which the student studies on his own but with the contiguous and non-contiguous support of the tutor. The learning material may, but as a rule does not, include specially prepared distance-education courses.

> Contract learning under the guidance of an expert in the particular field of study operationalizes the notion of individualization. It allows the mentor to develop educational alternatives responsive to the needs of diverse students and makes available academic programmes appropriate to the full range of motives and orientations toward knowledge and learning processes.
>
> (Coughlan 1980, p.3)

The feasibility and potentials of a general application of completely individualised distance study is being investigated at the FernUniversitat (Lehner & Weingartz 1985).

Student-tutor interaction

The type of course materials used exerts strong influence on both the roles and types of tutor-student interaction. The ´contract-learning` type of distance education evidently requires extensive personal communication, whereas - to take an extreme contrast - elementary teaching of mathematics is sometimes brought about by fully self-contained printed courses and correction of students´ assignments with largely pre-produced, sometimes computerised comments on expected mistakes, misunderstandings and questions.

On the basis of his analysis of distance education in relation to ´a number of contemporary teaching models` Bååth concludes:

o   Models with stricter control of learning towards fixed goals tend to imply, in distance education, a greater emphasis on the teaching material than on the two-way communication between student and tutor/institution.

o   Models with less control of learning towards fixed goals tend to make simultaneous communication between student and tutor/institution more desirable, this communication taking the form of either face-to-face or telephone contacts.

(Bååth 1982, p.15; cf. Bååth 1979)

This is no doubt an accurate observation of most types of distance education which include non-contiguous, mediated communication as an essential element, but it does not apply universally, for example not to the East-European type of distance education (cf. Chapter 1) which is strictly controlled to lead to prescribed goals. Here interaction between tutors and students (face-to-face) is nevertheless an essential characteristic. This heavy reliance on face-to-face interaction is also - as shown above - typical of much, but not all, of the Australian activity in the field of university distance study. It seems very doubtful whether these Australian activities preparing students for degree examinations should be classified as ´models with less control of learning towards fixed goals`.

Non-contiguous communication usually takes

place in writing, on the telephone or by computer.
Correspondence and telephone interaction are the
most common procedures applied. Whereas the former
can be - and very often is - strictly structured by
questions to be answered, problems to be solved,
translations to be made (but sometimes includes
essay writing and free exchanges of questions and
answers, opinions and criticism), telephone contacts
seem mainly to cater for question-and-answer service
and, particularly when conference telephoning is
applied, discussions. Audio cassette interaction
also occurs and seems to be particularly useful in
language teaching, speech training and in courses
for blind people. These and other methods, the
frequency and organisation of communication are
investigated in, for example, Bath 1980, Flinck
1978, Hathaway 1966, Holmberg 1985a (pp.87-102),
Stewart 1978, Valkyser 1981, Vincent 1982. On
information technology and media see below.

The traditional kind of non-contiguous
communication is correspondence, and there can be no
doubt that written two-way communication still pre-
dominates in distance education. It is also the
application of written communication in the form of
submission assignments with corrections and comments
that we know most about. Baath has investigated
this type of communication thoroughly. The following
extract illuminating its functions is taken from his
monograph of 1980:

The assignments for submission and their functions

The postal communication between student
and correspondence tutor is, as a rule,
induced by <u>assignments for submission</u>.....
According to MACKENZIE (1974), assignments
for submission hold a central position in
the Open University system of distance
education. They are, he maintains,
"...the only thoroughgoing and substantial
means open to the student to develop and
concentrate his thinking". A study of
mine reveals that representatives of
European correspondence schools teaching
at non-university levels also regard
assignments for submission as an extremely
important element in their teaching....

Table 2. Functions of assignments for submission, according to rankings made by European correspondence schools and the Open University.......
....

Functions	Rank Points(1)
1. To give the students effective feedback - help them to correct their mistakes and control their progress	91
2. To motivate the students, owing to the fact that the assignments for submission serve as sub-goals	58
3. To make it possible for the school to evaluate the students' achievements during the course, in order to be able to give each student help ("formative evaluation")	49
4. To give the instructor/tutor opportunity to motivate the students by giving them encouragement, praise etc.	38
5. To activate the students	37
6. To give the students opportunities for application and transfer of their knowledge	37
7. To make it possible for the school to evaluate the students' achievements and mark their solutions, in order to be able to give them certificates at the end of the study ("summative evaluation")	33
8. To give the school feedback - help it to find out how well its instruction works and in what ways the material should be revised	32

Functions	Rank Points(1)
9. To create opportunities for contact between students and school, in order to counteract students´ feelings of isolation	30
10. To give the students opportunities for survey, summing up and integrating various parts of the unit (or different parts of the course)	26
11. To focus the students´ attention on important learning objectives	14
12. To serve as a means for the students to revise the whole study unit	10
13. To teach in such a fashion that knowledge is retained, through practice in writing	5
14. Sent according to schedule, to compel the students to regular work	5
	465

(1) Rank points were calculated in the following way: A first ranking was given 5 points, a second ranking 4 points, etc., and a fifth ranking 1 point. Thus calculated, the maximum total of points possible of any of the functions would be 34 x 5 = 170 points (N = 34), and the maximum total sum of points 34 x (5+4+3+2+1) = 510. This sum indicates that a number of institutions did not distribute as many rankings as they were allowed to do.

(Bååth 1980, p.31)

There can be little doubt that the functions mentioned apply to the non-contiguous tutor-student interaction that occurs also by other means than the written word. At an advanced level the communication evidently serves the purpose of giving students opportunities to develop their thinking and of benefiting from tutors´ criticism.

There is evidently similar thinking behind the use of face-to-face sessions in distance education. They are useful as opportunities to consult subject specialists (cf. the East German word for them: Konsultationen) and to exchange views with tutors and fellow-students as well as to benefit from tutors´ expositions and criticism of work done. Since cognitive study objectives, those affective objectives which are concerned with academic socialisation (unprejudiced search etc.), and some psychomotor objectives (skills in writing, drawing, calculating, typing etc.) are attained as well by non-contiguous methods (Childs 1965, Granholm 1971, Holmberg 1976), face-to-face interaction seems mainly suitable for:

o   practising psychomotor skills in laboratories and under similar conditions; also verbal skills through personal communication;

o   facilitating the understanding of the communication process and human behaviour;

o   encouraging attitudes and habits of relevance for the study;

o   mutual inspiration and stimulation of fellow students;

o   training in co-operation.

A question that is under debate is to what extent continuous face-to-face sessions should also, more or less as a matter of routine, be used for the purpose of securing cognitive learning by discussion and application of the knowledge acquired to themes brought up in direct contact with tutors and fellow students. Whereas one school of thinking finds face-to-face sessions essential, another finds them unnecessary and even, in some cases, harmful as they are felt to represent interference disturbing the individual study. In cases where course completion within a pre-determined period of time is a target, students using supplementary face-to-face sessions have often been found to be particularly successful.

To be profitable, combinations of distance and face-to-face tuition have proved to need complete integration based on systematic planning allocating the two approaches to well-defined tasks in the study process. Normally, personal consultations along the lines of Oxbridge tutorials and discussions in groups, organised and formed spontaneously, appear to be the most valuable supporting functions of face-to-face sessions apart from those that require special equipment (laboratories, machinery, computers, etc.).

One form of integrating distance study with face-to-face sessions that has been found profitable is running concentrated residential courses supporting individual distance study. These can help students over previously insurmountable difficulties, they can introduce and thereby facilitate the study of new parts of the distance course, they can inspire co-operation with fellow students and provide a pleasant academic atmosphere with motivational potentials. As they take place during concentrated periods, when an interruption is made in the individual distance study, they do not interfere with or disturb this.

Communication as characterising distance education

The background of the concern with communication in distance education, as in all other kinds of education, is the awareness that human beings, although learning individually, usually develop their thinking in an advantageous way by talking their concepts and ideas over with some partner. Premeditated communication of this kind in the form of correspondence or prepared telephone conversations, cannot reasonably be expected to be less valuable than chats.

The communication element is rightly considered a corner stone of distance education; the more it resembles conversations - naturally premeditated and well-prepared - the better. It is my contention that when real didactic conversation cannot take place it is the spirit and atmosphere of conversation that should - and largely do - characterise distance education.

Text elaboration has something of a conversational character when it means thinking aloud. Cf. Lewis, who rejects any contrasting of ´conversational activity with more solitary activities such as private reasoning and silent reading`, which he characterises as `internalised conversation`. `As we mull things over quietly and in solitude, we are actually holding a conversation with ourselves` (Lewis 1975, p.69).

If we accept that this elaborative text processing and `internalised conversation` represents a useful learning strategy it is logical to draw conclusions from this to a teaching strategy. In its simplest form this would imply causing students to apply an appropriate extent of text elaboration to their learning. This leads to what I have called a style of guided didactic conversation likely to influence students´ attitudes and achievements favourably.

My theory (on which see Chapter 8) implies that the character of good distance education resembles that of a guided conversation aiming at learning and that the presence of the typical traits of such a conversation facilitates learning. The distance-study course and the non-contiguous communication typical of distance education are seen as the instruments of a conversation-like interaction between the student on the one hand and the tutor and counsellor of the supporting organisation administering the study on the other. There is constant interaction (`conversation`) between the supporting organisation (authors, tutors, counsellors) and the student, simulated through the students´ interaction with the pre-produced courses and real through the written and/or telephone inter-action with their tutors and counsellors.

Communication is thus seen as the core of distance education.

Information technology and media

The importance given to communication raises the question with whom or what distant students communicate. In correspondence and telephone inter-action there is a human being at the other end, but this is by no means the rule in computerised communication. Here communication with a programme, which may well offer good answers, comments and suggestions, is often what is provided. This applies to normal practice as far as both main-frame computers and micro-computers are concerned (Lampikoski 1984, O´Shea 1984). Evidently this may be in order in courses in which there are indisputably correct answers and no need for unforeseen discussions. Under these circumstances view-data computer systems (videotex) may become useful media for interactive teaching by combined use of TV and the telephone. Videodisc systems appear promising as they can allegedly cater not only for audio and video presentation, but also for interactive teaching by computer programmes for branching.

In normal academic study communication with a programme is not enough, however; here discussions of individual problems, approaches and solutions are important. Information technology can be helpful here, too, for instance through combinations of microcomputer technology and telephone communication. Conference tutorials by telephone and combined with microcomputer technology have proved successful, thus in the Open University innovatory technique called CYCLOPS (McConnell 1982). Useful studies of technology in distance education are brought together in Bates 1984.

The application of so-called telefax and modern text processing of the type used by newspapers (when contributions are typed by a correspondent at a distance from the printing-office to where it is transmitted electronically and where it may be changed or edited) may also be applied to bring about rapid correction and other two-way traffic in distance education. Such developments would seem to belong to the most essential educational endeavours of today as they would facilitate individual and autonomous learning based on mediated dialogue allowing for critical discussion, i.e. a type of really liberal education irrespective of subject areas chosen and this without the delay usually unavoidable in non-contiguous two-way communication.

The last mentioned aspect is important as the great weakness of distance education has in most cases been the slowness of the communication process caused by the correspondence method dominating this kind of education. For a student assignment to be sent by the student, received by the supporting organisation, corrected, commented on and returned to the student so that he/she receives it within a week is considered remarkably quick and represents a turn-around time that many distance-education institutions (and post offices) seem unable to achieve. Counselling distance students is subject to the same delay. So far mainly telephone communication has been used to overcome this difficulty, but as in most cases problem solving in writing, essays and translations are the objects of communications, the telephone is mainly a supplementary teaching medium and remains so even if it is combined with tele-transmission of written elements, drawings etc.

The most common use of the computer concerns off-line systems. Fully developed systems of this kind like CADE (Hermods, Sweden) make use of a computer off-line for the correction of and commenting on replies to multiple-choice questions with carefully selected distractors (Bååth & Månsson 1977). An off-line computer system which allows the free rendering of replies in the form of numbers has been developed at the FernUniversität (CMA). The numbers are 'read' by the computer, not by 'mark sensing', but by the numbers being produced through markings in columns of numbers provided. Thus, there is no choice between different solutions suggested (Möllers 1981). The students create their own answers (numbers).

This off-line use of the computer in most cases causes a reduction of the turn-round time of student assignments, but as students' solutions as well as the corrections and comments are sent by mail it does not lead to immediate communication.

Information technology is applied in distance education not only for the purpose of providing for interaction with tutors (or fellow-students) but also for the one-way presentation of learning matter. The value of TV and video recordings for demonstration of laboratory experiments, medical operations and other processes for which visual rather than verbal approaches are required, cannot be doubted. Here belong graphics whose constructions are shown by animation techniques. Video discs would seem to offer some possibilities here with their large storage capacity coupled with freeze-frame and fast-search equipment. Maybe the same will be attained by video cassettes. Further development work on this would seem to be called for as it can evidently improve motion-picture presentation.

However, I doubt if modern information technology has much value for purely verbal messages. At the present time when the presentation of text and graphics on a screen instead of on paper is becoming more and more common (videotex, teletext), we should ask ourselves if or to what extent this is a desirable development. It undoubtedly is desirable when urgent, really new information is provided, i.e. information not available in books or articles (the parallel with information about rates of exchange, airplane bookings etc. is illuminating), but in other cases I am inclined strongly to doubt its value. The same applies to computer print-outs.

For teaching purposes the presentation of verbal subject matter in print appears in all respects decidedly superior to screen (computer) presentation: it is easier to read, it facilitates leafing and browsing and it is open to all sources available, not only such as have been deemed suitable by decision makers for computer storage or micro-fiche presentation. There can be no doubt that for all serious study the reading of printed material will remain a prime medium, often in distance education in combination with audio recordings.

The application of media in distance education varies considerably. Data from a FernUniversitat comparative study which is to be reported on in Chapter 7 will demonstrate this.

Organisation - an attempted typology

In the preceeding discussion distance education of broadly speaking three different types have been referred to. They are:

1. correspondence schools and other public and private organisations outside the educational services normally provided by society; their ultima ratio is teaching at distance per se and their basic characteristic is the distance-teaching mode irrespective of types of target groups or aims, formal or informal education or training; they may meet the demands in their field of a whole nation or of a large or small segment of a state or community

2. distance-teaching universities and schools which are part of the educational establishment, but differ from other educational organisations by teaching at a distance and by offering special facilities for part-time study and further education beside students´ other commitments; they normally claim national coverage

3. extension departments of traditional universities and other educational institutions which offer ´extra-mural` study facilities for formal or informal distance study beside their basic activity; usually no attempt is made to cover whole countries or serve large populations:

Australia with universities, colleges of advanced education and colleges of technical and further education (TAFE), teaching both at a distance and face to face, offers special applications. The organisation of this double provision has been given some attention in the distance-education debate. According to Guiton

Four idealised models of organisational structure in dual-mode institutions can be defined:

o   Segregated. Specialist internal and specialist external staff in each subject. One Faculty of External Studies in competition with several internal schools. Decentralised student support by regional study centres.

o   Integrated. Each subject prepared and taught in both internal and external modes by a single member of staff. A central External Studies Department provides administrative services. Student support by mandatory attendances on campus.

o   Articulated. Course development by teams. Spin off in the form of internal use of course materials. No separate external studies organisation. Radiated student support by campus based services and through study centres.

o   Interlocked. Each subject prepared in internal and external modes by a single academic faculty member with a specialist distance education adviser. A central External Studies Department provides academic and administrative services. Radiated provision of student support from campus to students´ homes.

(Patrick Guiton, Director of the Extra-Mural department of Murdoch University in Western Australia in a handout at the ICDE conference in Melbourne in 1985).

A fourth category may consist of organisations which from their inception use different modes of teaching and on the basis of needs, aims and practicability apply face-to-face and distance teaching separately and conjunctly in a way sometimes to blur the distinctions between these two modes. Maybe Deakin University in Australia can be said to represent this category? (1)

Whereas organisations of type 1 tend mainly to engage external subject specialists and otherwise work with what can be described as only a skeleton organisation of its own as far as academic staff is concerned, those of type 2 tend to build up full academic facilities of their own and those of type 3 largely rely on their mother organisations (universities etc.) to provide subject-matter specialists (within type 3 the University of Queensland in Australia is an exception, however). As a rule the former two represent what has been described above as the large-scale approach, whereas type 3 usually offers small-scale services.

In formal education, particularly for university degrees, organisations of type 1 sometimes function as service institutions to governmental authorities or universities. In these cases they may be relied on to develop courses and provide tuition preparing students for university degrees. In a very successful scheme of this sort starting in 1952 and already referred to in Chapter 4 above, Hermods in Sweden, co-operating with individual professors and university departments, arranged distance study at the university level in a number of subjects, developing courses and providing distance tuition, supplementary residential courses, counselling facilities etc. The Swedish universities took over the examination duties. This proved a successful scheme relieving the universities of the necessity of organising distance study at the same time as they retained the responsibility for standards. It made national coverage and a large-scale approach feasible.

This experience indicates a generally applicable economical possibility to organise university distance study of the large-scale type. What is required is a small specialised institution which:

o   engages course authors and other subject specialists from among the academic staff of existing universities

o   provides editorial service, expertise
     on didactics, media and communication

o   arranges course development inclusive of
     formative evaluation (developmental
     testing), printing and other technical
     production (not necessarily within the
     organisation but also or exclusively
     through the use of commercial companies)

o   organises and runs counselling activities,
     the commenting and correction of student
     papers, tutoring on the telephone as well
     as any supplementary face-to-face sessions
     found desirable

o   keeps constant contact with co-operating
     universities, arranges examination oppor-
     tunities, etc.

o   takes responsibility for distribution,
     warehousing and general administration.

Setting up an organisation of this service type is
evidently less complicated and much less costly than
setting up a full distance-study university.
Whether it is an acceptable choice or not will
depend on the general conditions of university
education in the countries concerned.

Special distance-study organisations co-
operating with traditional universities are, for
instance, - apart from Hermods - the French Centre
National d´Enseignement par Correspondance and, in
some respects, the British National Extension
College (NEC). The latter organisation prepares
external students for London University degrees on a
highly individual basis. Whereas Hermods provides
its university students with pre-produced courses,
NEC seems not to do so, but to allocate individual
tutors to its students. The tuition occurs in
writing, on the telephone and by means of face-to-
face meetings (El-Bushra 1973).

Other forms of co-operation between universities and specialised distance-study institutions
are to be found in the English Flexistudy system,
whereby a college or other tutorial body buys
pre-produced distance-study courses from a
course-producing organisation and provides tuition
on the basis of these courses (Green 1979,
Sacks 1980). A service and research organisation
that partly corresponds with this type of

organisation is Deutsches Institut für Fernstudien at the University of Tübingen in West Germany. It develops and evaluates courses for use by other educational bodies and also does independent research (Rebel 1984).

The organisational structure has bearings on the conditions and practice of distance education as will be shown in Chapter 7.

Evaluating distance education

Educators and society at large find it increasingly important to evaluate the various contributions made to education. This is because of the general desire to safeguard the highest possible educational quality and also to make sure that money is invested in a way that yields the highest possible educational output. Evaluation is a general educational concern with some special implications for distance study.

The term 'evaluation' denotes different things in different contexts. Sometimes it refers to the assessment of students for the purpose of awarding marks; sometimes to the judgment of complete educational systems. The evaluation of distance-study courses and their tutorial support is an important concern in distance education.

A good deal of both theoretical study and practical work has gone into the evaluation of distance education, both of a formative type (to improve courses and tuition) and of a summative type (to describe and provide a kind of product declaration). The bases of evaluation are learning objectives, performance standards and achievement tests on the one hand, students' and specialists' opinions on the other hand. A special concern is the cost-benefit relation in distance education.

A survey of the problems of distance-education evaluation with references to various studies made is included as Chapter 6 in Holmberg 1985a and is dealt with in some depth by Holt and Evans in Open Campus August 1985. Cf. also Keegan 1986 (part 5).

NOTES

1. As explained in Chapter 4 above Deakin is a dual-mode institution offering both distance and on-campus teaching. The arguments in favour of the dual-mode approach stated by the Vice Chancellor of Deakin, Professor Fred Jevons, at the ICDE conference in Melbourne in 1985 are these:

1. Integration of distance education with the other teaching and administrative activities of the institution.
2. Spillover effects from distance education which may raise the quality of the other teaching activities.
3. Credibility. It is easier to argue for parity of esteem between the two modes.
4. Economies of scale when materials prepared for distance education students are used also by on campus students.
5. Reluctance of governments to start new institutions.
6. Teaching is enriched by being conducted in association with research.
7. New technologies lead to convergence of distance education and on campus education.

(Quoted from conference handout)

Chapter 6

PERVASIVE THEMES

Several of the characteristics that have been
considered most important by distance educators up
to the present times are indicated in early
documents, as evident from those referred to and
quoted in Chapters 2 and 3. Here belong potentials
for individualisation and for developing students'
independence in learning situations, respect for and
attention to adult student's maturity, and the
prominence of mediated communication. Interestingly
enough, the simulated conversation-like communication discussed in Chapter 5 is part and parcel of
the nineteenth-century Methode Rustin, which
actually includes conversation in a more literal
sense than later conversation theory (cf. Holmberg,
Schuemer & Obermeier 1982 and Pask 1976).

Controversial issues

In spite of this base in early distance
education some of the general educational principles
and a number of other issues seem to divide
distance-education practitioners and theorists and
in any case indicate partly different thinking
leading to different procedures. Among these issues
- in fact representing not only sometimes
contradictory approaches but also choices to be made
in different situations and with different
target-groups in mind - the following seem to be of
particular importance.

o Individualisation and student autonomy

Individualisation was expressly mentioned by
Lighty in 1915. He says that it would be 'folly' to
class those as failures who do not complete their
courses (op.cit., Mackenzie & Christensen 1971

p.21). He, like some later distance educators, leaves it to the individual student to decide when he/she has satisfied his/her original purpose. Cf. Delling 1975. This logically leads to students being offered a considerable degree of flexibility and autonomy in making decisions about their study. The practice of distance education shows, however, that these principles are far from always adhered to. In some cases close parallelism and resemblance to ordinary schools and universities have been considered advantageous and students have been made to follow not only the curricula laid down by those in charge of the organisations but also detailed timetables.

To those in favour of this kind of control of students, William Lighty´s acceptance of students´ rights themselves to decide what and how much to study must be unacceptable. Much of the public education that is provided today through the distance-teaching universities and in decentralised distance-teaching activities of individual schools and universities endeavours - though to differing extents - to control students. This is meant to be in the students´ best interest as evident from the following extracts from a paper concerned with ´getting the mixture right` by two modern distance educators:

> ...if a system has, as its chief priority, respect for the freedom and autonomy of the individual student, it will allow him to begin a course of study whenever he chooses and to finish it at his convenience. The student paces himself and there are no external constraints although the good correspondence school, whose model this is, will have a system of written reminders, encouraging phone calls and even financial incentives to incite him to keep at it. Nevertheless the drop out, or non-completion rate, with such a free approach is usually horrendous (over 50 per cent) if the students are humans rather than angels. In the nineteenth century, when correspondence schools began, the idea of the survival of the fittest was more acceptable than it is today and most modern remote learning systems, knowing that many of their students join them with feelings of educational inadequacy, are concerned to

do everything in their power to prevent the student dropping out with his sense of failure reinforced.

The usual way to encourage students to continue with a course is to provide some form of pacing, i.e. to introduce into the system a series of events taking place at fixed times which become deadlines for the students to meet`.

(Daniel & Marquis 1979, p.34)

This should be compared with what another leading distance educator of today, R. M. Delling, has to say. In an article written in 1975 he asks a number of awkward questions directed at the prescriptive systems which do not `take the "age of citizen" seriously`. Among his questions are these:

...whatever gives educational politicians, planners, and educationists the right to the absolute decision as to how long an educational process may last? ...Why should the learners in distant study not learn according to their own fashion but according to the fashion forced upon them...?

(Delling 1975, pp.58-59)

It is typical of distance education that it opens unique possibilities for teaching and learning adapted to individual needs, wishes and conditions. It seems logical to use these facilities without imposing unnecessary restraints, which may be unavoidable in classroom situations. Possible harmful consequences of students´ inability to complete a study programme or to do so in what seems to be a reasonable period of time should not be underestimated, however. Other methods than strict control of students can be used to counteract any consequences of this kind, though.

The basic question here is if students are considered capable of looking after themselves or whether they need guardians. In other words are those organising distance education responsible for students´ welfare or are the students themselves responsible for this? To the mature student complete liberty may lead to the most desirable type of welfare. This, of course, means that students are allowed to decide what to do, when and how to do it and precludes any pacing imposed on students. If students themselves decide what is good for them they are evidently entitled to complete only part of a course and to drop out if and when they wish to. This means that completion rates indicate degrees of success only in the cases when the students concerned aim at course completion, examinations or degrees rather than idiosyncratic acquisition of knowledge or education per se.

The question arises what is really meant by student autonomy in distance education and to what extent distance study is really individual. There can be no doubt that distance study is normally a highly individual activity that the student goes in for at home on his own and usually in his spare time. It is also evident that it is an exercise in independence. This independence usually covers the planning, timing and carrying out of individual study. The independence of distant students is often limited to the completion of study tasks decided on by others than the students themselves, however. This need not be so as there are procedures which allow students to influence or even independently to decide not only how they are to study but also what. Constructive approaches engaging the students in the selection of study objectives have been developed both by Potvin 1976 and Ljoså & Sandvold 1976. Potvin 'denies the institution and the tutor the right to prescribe what the learner should learn and how he is to learn it' (Potvin 1976, p.30).

The main reason why student autonomy and possibilities for individualisation are often considered something of a guideline for distance education is, of course, that on the whole the distant students are adults. Combining study with other commitments raises particular problems which the adult student has to master. This is undoubtedly a difficult thing to achieve and, it is argued, can be expected only of mature people capable of independent decisions. The trend towards student autonomy is noticeable also in supervised correspondence education for children, of whom no initial independence whatsoever is expected. Tomlinson, Coulter & Peacock 1985 p.40, illuminating work in Western Australia, stress that 'a home tutor will supervise all lessons and at various stages take an active part in the child's learning activities. The second [expectation] is that over the six or seven years of schooling the child will become increasingly independent'.

Distant students´ views of themselves is of interest in this context. An investigation of these has been made by Göttert 1983, who reports on an interview study of more than 500 FernUniversitat prospective and real students. These ´saw themselves as more competitive, achievement oriented and assertive` than the average general population and student groups investigated (Gottert 1983). This may well apply also to other distant students than those of the FernUniversität, but for a fruitful discussion of the application of principles conducive to and in harmony with students´ autonomy some differentiation would seem to be necessary.

Students who have decided to pass an examination, acquire a degree or professional competence as quickly as possible are usually willing to accept and follow rather detailed plans leading them to their goal. Those students, on the other hand, who are entirely intrinsically motivated and study more to satisfy intellectual and scholarly interest than with a view to acquiring a document testifying to their academic or professional competence are no doubt less inclined to follow paths prescribed by others than themselves. This differentiation leads to consequences of various kinds, for instance for the demands on and the development of course materials. It evidently also has bearings on the consideration of what is usually called the drop-out problem.

Drop out indicates failure or, in any case, partly unsuccessful study in the cases when students have decided to study for the purpose of completing a study programme in a specified period. Then they either succeed or they fail. In such cases we have reason to talk about drop-out problems in distance education. Under other circumstances this is not the case. When distance-education programmes are used by individual students who do not declare either their ultimate goals (which may be self-actualisation rather than the acquisition of competence) or the period over which they intend to spread their study, it is far from easy to say for certain whether non-completion means interruption for a time, or drop out in the sense of failure, or even entirely accords with the students´ intentions and plans. This is evidently what Lighty had in mind when in this context he described the identification of drop-out with failure as folly. This reservation does not only apply to purely academic study at an advanced level but also to the study of practical subjects of importance in job situations. The well-established accountant who takes a course in automatic data processing in order to get to know its basic principles and terminology so that he may be able to communicate with computer staff may well reach his goal by thoroughly reading the first few course units, submitting solutions of assignment problems based on these and, as far as the rest of the course is concerned, limiting himself to browsing and looking up items of special interest to him. This situation is highlighted by a reply given by a successful inventor and head of a large company to a question as to why he had not completed his course

> I am a busy man. I took this course to
> learn how to solve a certain problem in
> advanced physics. When I learned that,
> I stopped sending in lessons.

> (James & Wedemeyer 1960, p.20)

It would be unrealistic to assume that all distant students are intellectually and emotionally well equipped for autonomous study. Nevertheless, Gottert´s findings seem to indicate trends of relevance when due attention has been paid to different types of study motivation and causes for study.

While some distance educators both find it extremely important that distance education should as far as possible be based on and develop student autonomy and regard it as a realistic assumption that these claims can be properly met by means of suitable procedures (Moore 1983, Wedemeyer 1981, etc.), there are, in fact, others who do not seem to pay much attention to the potentials of distance education in this respect (Willen 1981, e.g.).

In my view it is important on the one hand to serve already autonomous learners, on the other hand to use distance education as a means to developing student independence (cf. the international comparative study reported on in Chapter 7). This includes respect for the learners whose decision rights are not questioned. When they are offered help and guidance it must be up to them to accept or reject the offer. This is by no means universally accepted, however.

There are different views of to what extent students should be given decision rights and/or be controlled by a teaching organisation. This seems basically to be a case of liberalism vs dirigisme (cf. the quotations from Daniel & Marquis and Delling above).

The philosophical background of individual-isation and student autonomy is analysed in Lehner & Weingartz 1985, who pay particular attention to on the one hand rationalism, on the other hand transpersonal psychology.

o Respect of students´ integrity vs interference to support them

There is a school of thinking that finds it tactless if tutors or other representatives of the supporting organisation, without being asked to, approach mature students with questions why they submit no work, why they work slowly etc. and offer them support (cf. the study reported on in Chapter 7). The view held means treating students as potentially independent people to whom it is left not only to decide, but expressly to state, if and to what extent they want support or advice. Practice implicitly testifies more frequently to this view than explicit principles.

The opposite view, as typically represented by the British Open University, implies that it is a social duty to interfere to prevent failure and to promote success. In this spirit Bååth, basing his presentation on well-known theoretical consider-ations, writes that ´it may be maintained that the tutor should get in touch, by mail or by telephone, with his newly enrolled students to

- be able to individualise his tuition with regard to the student´s previous "reinforcement patterns" (Skinner), or
- facilitate the student´s "mathemagenic activities" (Rothkopf), or
- be able to anchor the material of the first study units in the student´s individual previous knowledge and "cognitive structure" (Ausubel), or
- get an idea of the students´ comprehension of the basic concepts and principles of the course (Bruner), or
- establish a good personal relationship with the learner (Rogers).´

(Bååth 1984b, p.38)

The two approaches contrasted pose a problem to many liberal distance educators who would like to treat their students as mature, responsible personalities, but who still feel there is a duty spontaneously to support them and, if at all possible, prevent their experiencing failure.

o Behavioural objectives and the systems approach

Since the end of the 1960s there has been some discussion about the use of so-called behavioural objectives, i.e. specific decisions in advance about what kind of capabilities a course is to lead to and definitions of these capabilities in terms of behaviour stating not what the student is expected to know after the course but what he/she is expected to be able to do. It has been found to be good practice when defining objectives to avoid verbs of state, like know, understand, realise, grasp, master as these are particularly ambiguous. Verbal expressions of action, like recognise and state the symptom of, conduct experiment, demonstrate, do, enumerate, quote arguments for and against, prove, write an account of, report orally on, are examples of expressions found more acceptable in definitions of objectives.

Defining objectives in this way has on the one hand been found useful in making sure that courses concentrate on what students really need and that the influence of course authors´ idiosyncracies is minimised when irrelevant from students´ points of view. On the other hand there has been much criticism of this procedure. This criticism is often the outcome of a rejection of behaviourist psychology with its stimulus-response theory. However, many non-behaviourists seem to be prepared to use the technique developed for defining objectives without in any way accepting the mechanistic view of man seen as typical of behaviourism.

Not only doctrinaire reasons but also practical considerations have caused criticism of definitions of objectives. One objection is that it is almost impossible completely to avoid ambiguity in the formulation of objectives even if we exclusively use verbs of action (do, etc.) and avoid verbs of state (know, etc.). Even action verbs like deduce, recognise and solve have been shown to be ambiguous (Macdonald-Ross 1973, pp.35-36).

A further objection is that checking students´ attainments against learning objectives expressed in behavioural terms need not necessarily lead to any kind of proof that the objectives have or have not been attained. It is perfectly possible to make the right operation for the wrong reason, as shown by the following example borrowed from Lewis. Anyone who believes that .3 x .3 makes .9 (instead of .09) and that .2 x .2 makes .4 (instead of .04) will no doubt, on the basis of a false understanding, come to the conclusion that .3 x .5 = .15, which happens to be correct (Lewis 1974, p.16). It is evident that the operation is not enough; we must pay attention to the knowledge and understanding on which it is based.

Entirely behavioural objectives would seem to be in order in cases when accurate performance can be measured against them, which can be the case when there is an undisputably correct answer (certain points of grammar in a foreign language, for example, such as saying and writing <u>he takes</u>, <u>speaks</u>, etc. but <u>I take</u>, <u>you take</u>, etc.).

Once it is recognised that the application of detailed study objectives ´needs to be tempered with an understanding of its inherent deficiencies` (Macdonald-Ross 1973, p.47), there is evidently a strong case for their use in distance education. One reason for this is that distance-study courses are prepared well ahead of their use by students and thus give little scope for improvisations. There can be little doubt that specified learning objectives can serve useful functions as planning devices, as control instruments to be used by course developers and as eye-openers to these when they confront their pet subject areas with the needs of students. This is a rational approach in line with and part of educational technology described by Ripley Sims ´as a systematic way to design, produce, implement, evaluate, and improve a teaching-learning system`. Sims stresses the importance of integrating goal decisions with the other elements: ´...each phase is discussed separately, but there is a constant reminder of the interrelatedness among the phases. This assures a continuing awareness of the intergrative and iterative functioning of the phases when viewed as a whole. Thus, the interpretation is both analytical and synthetic, which is analogous to a <u>systems</u> approach in educational technology. Without this perspective, the principal focus may become blurred by some of the detail necessary for analysis and synthesis purposes` (Sims 1977, p.367).

If, on the other hand, distance education is to cater for entirely individual curricula, instead of providing pre-produced courses is to offer information about sources, advice on how to tackle them and facilities for non-contiguous communication between student and tutor on the topics of relevance to the individual student, then detailed objectives are not only out of place but unpracticable, at least until the student has decided on the curriculum to be followed. The quantitatively modest application that occurs of this kind of distance education (in the form of contract learning) was briefly commented on in Chapter 5 above.

The use of specified objectives is particularly thorny when such goals are concerned as transcend measurable cognitive and manipulative skills. Education and training sometimes aim at influencing attitudes, for instance making students critical readers or encouraging co-operation, understanding and empathy of relevance to the treatment of patients, clients etc. Professional socialisation belongs here. Religious and political education are particularly sensitive areas.

Intellectual honesty requires that any goals of this kind are made explicit. It is, on the other hand, doubtful if they should be expressed as behavioural objectives. In many cases this is simply impossible. The main reason why goals in this affective domain should be spelled out is that it is important for students to be able to protect themselves against indoctrination. The first pre-requisite then is that they are made aware of any wish to influence them.

While this thinking is hardly ever openly rejected, it is often neglected in practice. Special caution is advisable in religious and political education, in social sciences and philosophy.

o Attention-directors and other learning aids in courses

Techniques have been developed to direct students´ attention to important issues, to considering and searching for solutions. Rothkopf´s questions aimed at promoting ´mathemagenic-positive` behaviour belong here (Rothkopf 1970). Whereas much research supports the use of questions as attention-directors and it is said to be advocated by common sense (cf. Macdonald-Ross 1979) some scholars are rather negative. This would seem to apply to Weingartz, who considers formal text criteria fairly insignificant in relation to the basic text design, which may start out from problems to be solved and thus support problem learning, or may simply present ready-made systems of knowledge for reproductive learning, and even more to Marton, who fears that all kinds of attention-directors may avert students' interest from the content to the technical aspects of the reading process, thus encouraging surface learning and leading to neglect of deep structure learning (Weingartz 1981, Marton 1979).

To judge from practice it seems as though most distance educators are open-minded when considering this issue and tend to think that questions merely concerning facts, wordings and examples provided in the text may encourage what Marton calls surface learning, but that questions causing students to think independently, to formulate their thoughts and relate these to the text are not only radically different from the questions bearing on the wordings of texts, but would also seem to be instruments for encouraging problem learning and deep-structure study.

Similar discussions apply to the facilitation of readability and the applications of research findings on readability (Taylor 1977, Groeben 1972, Langer-Schulz von Thun & Tausch 1974, etc. summarised in Holmberg 1985a, Chapter 3.6). Readability formulae using word length, word frequency, sentence length and similar measures to predict reading difficulty have been used with some success. In a critical study of language in texts Macdonald-Ross comes to the conclusion that - in spite of the problems known - a ´readability "filter" is...more reliable than the exercise of unaided human judgment' (Macdonald-Ross 1979, p.5). He refers to what is known about

> the clear relationship between readability and learner acceptability (Klare et al 1955), between readability and efficiency of reading (Klare et al 1957). Klare and Smart (1973) found a rank-order correlation of 0.87 between the readability level of correspondence material and the probability that students would send in all their lessons (with length held constant). Such decisively clear-cut field results are not to be put aside lightly.
>
> (Macdonald-Ross ibidem, p.4)

o Organisation of course development

Two approaches can be contrasted. One implies that an individual author co-operates with an editor who takes the main responsibility for the educational and technical methods. The other approach foresees a large course team for each course with authors, other subject specialists, media specialists (for print, radio, TV, etc.), artists, editors, etc. This latter type of organis- ation is advantageous in providing for the best expertise available for all the various tasks involved (cf. Perry 1976, p.77, who regards the course-team approach as ´one of the most important and far-reaching concepts of the Open University which, it seems probable, will become more and more widely used all over the world`.) However, the course-team approach may lead to a de-personalised style of presentation contrary to the style of didactic conversation and may favour the presentation of learning matter as ready-made systems rather than as guides to problem-solving. Cf. Weingartz 1980, pp.167-169. To what extent these effects occur or are avoidable is uncertain, although there are signs that few of the courses created by course teams are based on problem-solving approaches (Weingartz op.cit). On organisational models for course development generally see Holmberg 1983a and Kaufman 1982. It is evident that there is no unanimity about either the course-team or the author-editor approach (cf. the debate in <u>Teaching at a Distance 16</u>, initiated by Michael Drake).

o Mediated two-way communication between students and tutors

The need for contact with other human beings in all serious endeavour is usually the implicit cause why most distance educators insist on regular communication, <u>nolens volens</u> usually of a mediated non-contiguous type. On the declared purposes of this communication cf. Chapter 5.

There are different types of mediated two-way communication, however. There is the student- initiated contact, which many organisations appear to encourage but which is usually of modest scope, and there is communication initiated by assignments given to students. The latter can include penetrating exchanges of arguments, tutors´ suggestions for further reading, comments on field work and experiments - all in writing, on the telephone or, though rarely, on audio tape - but can also simply consist of questions or problems, the answers and solutions of which are ticked off as correct or wrong with or without explanatory tutor comments. Practise shows that distance-teaching organisations can be divided into two groups, those which in most cases merely correct assignments and those which insist on teaching by comprehensive comments.

This dichotomy implicitly recalls the approaches identified by William Perry 1970. To regard learning as acquiring the capacity to provide a number of replies that are correct (stage 1) is a primitive view that higher-level students give up fairly early. The reason why they do so is that they realise - through varied reading - that in many cases there is no such thing as an answer or solution that is absolutely right. This relativism (stage 2) represents an important experience, on the basis of which students may reach conclusions and positions of their own (stage 3).

The issue here is evidently if correct answers are considered enough, in which case spoon-feeding or presentation of given truths in larger doses may be acceptable. If, on the other hand, problem-solving approaches are important, then pluralistic approaches are required, making students aware of different interpretations, views, positions and possibly acceptable or defensible conclusions as well as requiring them to suggest solutions of their own. While there are few explicit protagonists of the former approach there is much empirical evidence showing that it is implicitly accepted in more than a few cases.

Other issues connected with mediated two-way communication concern the frequencies of interaction (Bååth, 1980), the turn-round time for students' papers to be duly commented on and returned (Rekkedal 1983) and the importance of personal approaches. The insistence on short turn-around time is nothing new. As early as 1886 William Harper wrote that student papers are to be ´promptly returned with all errors corrected, and questions answered; and with special suggestions, suited to each individual case` (op.cit. MacKenzie & Christensen 1971, p.8). How this concern is dealt with in different organisations to some extent reflects the view held of students, as responsible clients with a right to be served well and quickly or as subordinates who have to await their tutors' convenience or that of an administrative apparatus.

The frequency problem is related both to what is desirable and helpful from the students' point of view and to the question of pacing.

Communication based on assignments can be merely matter-of-fact without any really personal element. Many distance educators - among them the present author - consider such impersonal correction and commenting a waste of valuable opportunities. If personal rapport is established, students are likely to enjoy the learning more and to be more successful than otherwise. Cf. the theory of guided didactic conversation briefly outlined in Chapter 5.

A study by Rekkedal of the consequences of a personal tutor-counsellor system including intro-ductory letters in which the tutor-counsellors introduce themselves to their students, short turn-round times for assignments and frequent telephone contacts with students supports this view. The study comprised a comparison between an experimental group offered these services by a personal tutor-counsellor while studying 3 - 11 courses of a course combination leading to a professional qualification and a control group following the usual pattern of the school concerned (NKI in Oslo).

> The main difference between the treatment of the experimental group and the control group was that the experimental students communicated with one personal tutor integrating administrative, teaching and counselling functions, which normally are separated.
>
> (Rekkedal 1985, p.9)

Statistically significant differences were found between the two groups. 'The students in the experimental group had a higher completion rate, they were more active in their studies and completed a larger number of study units and courses during the experimental period' (Rekkedal 1985, p.13).

There can be no doubt that in spite of the success of this personal style some distance educators prefer a more neutral, less personal approach avoiding intervention in students' learning situation. This may be due to academic tradition or to a conscious choice. Cf. the discussion above of the respect of mature students' integrity.

o The role of face-to-face contact

The presentation given in Chapter 5 about different views of the role of face-to-face sessions indicates a kind of ´middle-of-the-road` practice in using concentrated residential courses and Oxbridge tutorials as supplements of ´pure` distance education.

In spite of this there remains a basic controversy between those who are in favour of as much face-to-face contact as possible, and those who mainly rely on non-contiguous communication. To the former distance education is merely a substitute for face-to-face interaction when this is not available and learning is seen as something of a social activity. (1) To the latter learning is basically individual (2) and distance education has consider-able potentials of its own, different from, but not inferior to traditional types of education (cf. Holmberg 1985a, Chapters 1 and 2).

o The rationale of distance education

The very rationale of distance education can be controversial. Sometimes distance education is introduced to increase the number of places for students in certain programmes or to offer extended adult-education or further-education services. Lifelong learning and recurrent education in the spirit of Faure et al. 1972 are _desiderata_ which may be practicable through distance education. In other cases distance education is preferred for financial reasons, as its cost-benefit relations are con-sidered particularly favourable (cf. Holmberg 1985a, Chapter 7). Interest in educational innovation, methodological concerns, wishes to improve social equality and/or to serve individual learners are other impetuses of importance. Cf. the discussion at the beginning of Chapter 4 about the reasons behind the creation of the distance-teaching universities.

The question of the basic character of distance education belongs here. Is distance education nothing but a vehicle of distribution, or is it a type of education in its own right that ´can only be described and analysed to a limited extent using traditional educational terms` (Peters 1983, p.96)? The large-scale and small-scale approaches of, for example, the British Open University and the Australian University of New England are cases in point.

The former implies rather radical deviations

from the traditions of university education. Courses and services for large numbers of students are developed and offered by groups of subject specialists, course designers, media specialists and tutors etc. There is a division of labour based on each team member´s expertise. Economies of scale are attained by large editions of courses developed. Here distance education, mainly relying on contiguous communication, appears as a type of education in its own right.

The latter, on the other hand, favours more traditional procedures and often includes the maximum amount of face-to-face interaction possible. It makes use of distance-education distribution techniques for some of its teaching, which is otherwise characterised by a certain closeness between author/tutor and student.

Both approaches can claim that they represent individualisation. Cf. Thorpe 1979b p.1, who stresses that ´in the Open University the course teams provide the reading material (texts, broadcasts, kits) for hundreds or thousands of students in general and the course tutors and tutor-counsellors teach the students as individuals`.

Summing up

The pervasive themes and the issues discussed illustrate momentous approaches to distance education. Some of them have played a part in theory and practice since the time of the pioneers and were referred to in Chapters 1-3; others are of a more recent date. The views held of issues of this kind are largely decisive for the way distance education is applied. The discussion of them provides a framework within which any theory of distance education must find a base.

The divergent views discussed in this and earlier chapters could have been presented in a number of different ways. In the interest of discerning awareness the following dichotomies, although in part overlapping and listed in arbitrary order, may be fruitful:

o   Adapability to individual students´ family and job situation vs institutional rules

o   Students as respected clients vs students under orders

o   Individual study vs class or group learning

o   Cognitivism vs   behaviourism   and/or
     ´industrialisation`

o   Large-scale vs small-scale approaches

o   Student   autonomy   vs   dependence   on
     authority

o   Respect for students´ integrity vs social
     duty to extend uninvited support

o   Flexibility as desired by individual
     students vs confinement to prescribed
     curricula, pacing and course completion

o   Customer orientation and student friend-
     liness vs control

o   Exclusively non-contiguous communication
     vs use of   supplementary   face-to-face
     contacts, consistently or for   certain
     purposes

o   Information technology   vs   entirely
     personal communication

o   Problem learning vs learning of knowledge
     canons

o   Strategies for deep learning vs procedures
     possibly encouraging surface learning

o   Pluralism vs reliance on one approach

o   Self-contained courses   vs   study-guide
     courses

o   Personal vs less personal approaches

o   Conversational   style   and   distance
     education as didactic conversation   vs
     handbook presentation

o   Distance education in its own right vs
     distance education as a vehicle of
     knowledge distribution.

NOTES

1. Cf. Perraton, who in 1974 wrote ´Learning
...is normally a social activity´ (Perraton 1974, p.
58) and in 1976 argued ´against the assumption of a
necessarily close link between correspondence
education and "individualised learning"`; he stated
´that most learning in the world is a group activity
and that the case for not doing things on a group
basis is the more difficult one to sustain`. The
last two sentences of this paper run like this:
´Old-fashioned correspondence education won´t do.
If it isn´t dead already, let´s kill it off as soon
as we can` (Perraton 1976, p.84).

2. Cf. Sims: ´...in whatever society, for
whatever purpose, by whatever means, under whatever
ideology, the essential objective in educating
processes is learning by an individual
learner...the methodologies or strategies employed
are only incidental to this end` (Sims 1977, p.4).

Chapter 7

A STUDY OF PRACTICE IN THE 1980s

The solutions and attempted solutions of the practical and more or less philosophical issues discussed above are illuminated through data collected in the course of an international study undertaken as the first step in a FernUniversität comparative investigation of distance education in the years 1983–1985. On the basis of 290 replies to a very comprehensive questionnaire, 203 of which were reasonably complete, a number of analyses were made. Full reports in German on this comparative study are available in Graff & Holmberg 1984, Doerfert 1984, Holmberg & Schuemer 1985, Neuhoff & Riechel 1985 and in Buckmann, Holmberg, Lehner & Weingartz 1985. An English-language summary is Holmberg 1985b.

Some general data

63.5% of the organisations which answered the questionnaire are public bodies, 30.5% are private organisations of different kinds and 6% belong to associations, churches and political groups etc. 39.8% of them are autonomous, whereas 60.2% are departments either of traditional schools or universities (37.2%) or parts of other organisations (23%). 79.4% have a centralised organisation with one centre as decision maker.

The data available seem to indicate that the number of public bodies engaged in distance education has grown considerably during the last few years (34.7% of them were founded after 1975). Only 2.5% of all the responding organisations starting after 1975 belong to the private sector.

There can be little doubt that the private distance-teaching organisations are underrepresented in the study, however. Whereas the data about the latest developments probably represent general tendencies, it is evident that comparatively few private organisations, particularly in the U.S., have answered the questionnaire.

The organisations answering the questionnaire together include about 1.3 million distant students. Most of the respondents have less than 5,000 students enrolled (70.3% of them) and their staffs include fewer than 100 people (78.8%).

The reasons why distance education is provided as well as the aims of the organisations differ somewhat in relation to the type of body in charge. The public distance-education organisations are largely concerned with university teaching and regard the opening of study opportunities to new target groups as their main task. This is what 66.5% of the respondents state. 42% stress further education as their main task, whereas 33.5% describe the increase of the number of places for students as their first priority. Surprisingly enough little attention is paid to the possibilities usually considered inherent in distance education for reducing costs. Only 7.5% refer to cost reduction as an aim. The introduction of innovations plays an important part among the private organisations, whereas the expansion of further-education facilities is the chief concern of 75% of the associations, churches etc.

A great number of media are being used inclusive of radio and TV programmes, audio recordings, telephone contacts, computerised teaching and learning and face-to-face sessions. The overwhelmingly dominant type of course presentation occurs in print, however. 95% of the respondents refer to their use of printed course materials, often along with other media.

36 out of 194 organisations state that they offer their students a choice between different media.

What reality these statements cover is far from evident. Questions to be asked are, for instance: To what extent do the individual media on their own present the learning matter? Are certain media combinations consistently used in some cases? Are some media used exclusively for special purposes or as optional supplements to print and writing only?

As to the use of face-to-face teaching in distance education four categories could be identified:

1. 8.6% of the respondents regard

face-to-face teaching as one of the main components of their teaching (category 1)

2. 24.9% include compulsory face-to-face sessions in their courses (category 2)

3. 49.2% offer to some small extent optional face-to-face sessions (category 3), whereas

4. 17.3% make no use whatsoever of supplementary oral teaching (category 4).

Interesting relations emerged between different types of organisations as to their use of face-to-face sessions. The table on page 85 represents the picture for the 197 organisations that provided information about their work in this respect.

43 out of 203 organisations offer study-centre facilities to their students. 27 of them supply audio- and/or video cassettes in these centres. Laboratories/workshops are provided by 57 out of 203 organisations; computer facilities (terminals, microcomputers) are used by 42 out of these 203 organisations, whereas other types of equipment are referred to by 54 of them.

77 organisations claim to develop their courses in course teams consisting of between 2 and 10 members. However, 20 organisations use course teams consisting of 3 members, 24 course teams consisting of 4 members.

Some 55% of the respondents state that they regard the combination of a pre-produced course and mediated two-way communication as the most important type of teaching. However, no less than 45% consider the pre-produced course to be the most important element, whereas only seven respondents describe the interaction between the learner and the supporting institution as the most important element. As few as ten respondents declare that they make use of study-guide courses, i.e. courses based on prescribed or suggested reading of texts not necessarily developed by the supporting organisation itself.

Course evaluation and systems evaluation are considered important by most respondents. Thus 73.6% of them state that they systematically evaluate their courses. 61.2% include the achievements of the students on assignments in this

Category	State-owned organisations	Official bodies (univers-ities etc)	Private companies	Private non-profit organisa-tions	Other types of organis-ation	No organis-ational character-isation
1	6 (12.2)	6 (8.0)	1 (2.9)	2 (8.3)	1 (8.3)	1
2	6 (12.2)	25 (33.3)	4 (11.8)	10 (41.7)	4 (33.3)	0
3	28 (57.1)	38 (50.7)	16 (47.1)	8 (33.3)	5 (41.7)	2
4	9 (18.5)	6 (8.0)	13 (38.2)	4 (16.7)	2 (16.7)	0
	49 (100.0)	75 (100.0)	34 (100.0)	24 (100.0)	12 (100.0)	3

evaluation, whereas practically all respondents make use of the experience of their tutors. Completion and drop-out figures are measured by about 75% of the respondents, whereas no less than 86.2% analyse the turn-round time of assignments submitted.

Different types of assignment formats and types of solution are used beside one another: 69% make use of forms to be filled in for solutions to problems and other assignment questions; 88% expect students to answer short open questions; 90% expect an essay; 73% use multiple-choice questions, which, however, are used by 64% of the users of these questions for certain types of content only.

Most respondents find it very important that students´ answers to and solutions of assignment questions and problems should be commented on by the correcting tutor. Thus 84% reject mere correction without comments. However, the comments actually provided seem to be very short, according to the replies half a page or less in 78% of all cases. The comments given are overwhelmingly written for the individual students (94%); only in 17% of all cases are pre-produced text modules used.

The turn-round time varies very much, between 1 and 90 days (median about 9 days). 86% of the respondents assume that their students are satisfied with the turn-around-time.

In replies to questions about the purposes of self-checking assignments distance-education institutions tend to stress the retention of facts (77%) and practice (71%); to develop critical approaches is the purpose in only 27% of the replies.

About 90% of the respondents have an organisation for counselling and student support. This service is mainly provided in writing (86%) and by telephone (78%). Audio-cassette correspondence occurs in 12% of the cases.

Almost half of the respondents state that they assign a personal counsellor (tutor-counsellor) to each student (48%). This is surprising as 62% of the respondents also state that there are different counsellors for different problems or areas and as 72% reply that students´ problems and questions are received centrally and then handed on to specialists. This seems to indicate that a number of facilities for counselling occurs. The distinctions between them are blurred, however.

Practically all institutions (95%) encourage students to approach counsellors and tutors; the percentage of the students who actually do this varies between 5 and 100% (median between 25 and 30%).

Counselling and other student-support services are available during office hours in 39% of all cases mentioned, constantly 27%, on weekdays after office hours 13%, and at weekends 7%; 14% refer to other kinds of accessibility.

Approaches to basic issues

To the controversial issues discussed in the preceding chapters the FernUniversitat study contributes some information of interest, thus on flexibility, student independence, customer orientation, i.e. student friendliness, and on the view of distance education as innovation.

Flexibility

A study of the flexibility of distance education as seen from the students' point of view shows that almost two thirds of the respondents allow their students to pace their study according to their personal possibilities and wishes. Thus 64.7% allow their students to submit assignments whenever they wish to.

In other aspects the respondents seem to allow their students less freedom to organise their study, however. Only 1.5% of them allow their students simultaneously

o   to start their study at any time that suits them and to submit assignments whenever it suits them

o   to decide if they wish to take part in face-to-face sessions or not

o   to choose between different media

o   to use, if and whenever it suits them, counselling and student-support services offered.

57.8% offer the students several although not all of the possibilities listed for their free choice.

Regrettably there can be no doubt that the replies given to the questionnaire provide a biased picture of reality in the respects mentioned. If a larger number of private organisations, for instance the American schools organised in the National Home Study Council, had answered the questionnaire, there would without any doubt whatsoever have been many more schools included in the study representing a high degree of flexibility.

To judge from the material collected, flexibility offered to students does not seem to be conducive to more success than strictly controlled study. On the contrary there is a negative correlation (rho = -.15)(1) between completion and the number of choices available to individual students.

On flexibility see further under ´student friendliness` below.

Student independence

It proved possible to identify two characteristic approaches to student autonomy in that some distance-teaching institutions largely expect and base their work on the assumed prevalence of students´ capacity to work independently, whereas others more endeavour to develop a degree of independence not expected to be of ordinary occurrence among new students. The criteria, on which this distinction is based, have been illustrated as shown on pp.92 - 93.

The distinctions made there are based on indices for

support of student independence	expectation of student independence
1. The main goal of the teaching is capacity to solve problems.	1. The main goal of the teaching is to transmit facts.
2. Examination requirements are directed towards problem solving.	2. Examination requirements are directed towards the reproduction of facts.
3. Learners are made to query statements etc. (in the learning material).	3. The pre-produced course material is is considered to be the most important course component.
4. Students take active part in research if the degree of support for student independence is very high.	4. It is left to the student to initiate contact with the supporting organisation.

5. Continuous contact is catered for in that the supporting organisations approach students from whom nothing has been heard for some time.

5. Tutor comments on assignments submitted are limited to what is considered absolutely necessary.

6. Counselling and tuition services are usually available also outside office hours.

The correlation between the two indices for support and expectation of student independence is rho = -.70 (p < .001).(2) The relatively high negative correlation results from the circumstance that the two indices contain some question-initiated statements which practically exclude each other (see, for instance, the first item of each of the above two lists).
    An analysis of the replies submitted reveal the following characteristics:

Support of student
independence

Expectation of student
independence

PRIORITIES

The commitment to social responsibility tends to have the following activity consequences:
- Innovation attempts as to organisation, teaching and student support
- Research
- Further education in the interest of equality
- Evaluation (courses, success and failure, etc.)

A basic liberal principle causes what can be described as a somewhat conservative attitude.
- There is little interest in modern, costly media
- General education is particularly stressed, frequently at university level.

CENTRAL INSTITUTIONAL CHARACTERISTICS

Teaching:
Organised attempts to improve the course materials (course teams, various didactic measures etc.)

Teaching:
Traditional course offer, usually as transmission of knowledge already known (rather than problem solving).

Student support:
Institutional interventions are regarded as moral duties. Student support is considered a core concern.

Student support:
An offer of services that may or may not be used.

The institutions that support students´ independence exert much more control over students than those which expect student independence from the beginning. Some significant correlations:

Organisations characterised by their support of independence

o   use the telephone much more frequently than the others: rho = .27 (p = .001) vs rho = -.18 (p = .01)

o   more frequently form course teams: rho = .24 (p < .001) vs rho = -.18 (p < .01)

o   favour group work among students more: rho = .33 (p < .001) vs rho = -.20 (p < .01)

o   tend more frequently continuously to check on students´ progress: rho = .33 (p < .001) vs rho = .20 (p < .01)

As to general measures of control (face-to-face sessions, achievement checking, work groups, strict structuring of courses with special procedures to facilitate the learning of texts and for counselling) the correlations are for support of independence rho = .41 (p <.001), for expectation of independence rho = .18 (p < .01). Similarly individual control (contacts with students, telephone counselling, individual counselling, much support) shows a correlation of rho = .29 (p < .001) for support of independence. There is no correlation for expectation of independence.
Course completion as an indication of success is favourably influenced by support of independence: rho = .34 (p < .001) vs rho = -.21 (p = .01).
As independence supporting and independence expecting organisations are not or only partly exclusive concepts as understood here, further differentiation is required. Thus it is necessary to

distinguish between highly supporting organisations,
little supporting (low support), little expecting
(low expectation) and highly expecting institutions;
each organisation studied could be assigned to one
of these four groups.

The first two groups, i.e. those supporting
independence, include 60% of the organisations
studied against 40% of organisations expecting
independence. There are only modest differences as
to support and expectation between the two middle
groups, i.e. those representing low support and low
expectation respectively. Correlations with other
variables (such as achievements` variables) supply
the reasons for the differentiation between them.

The four groups differ significantly with
respect to the completion rates of the organisations
(Chi 2 = 12.87; df = 3; p < .01): 3

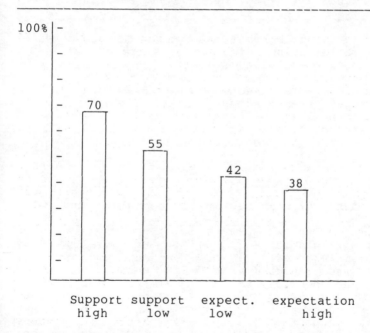

The figures show the proportion of organisations
with completion rates above the median of the total
distribution.

The data presented would seem to be of some
interest in relation to the discussion of student
autonomy in Chapter 6 and elsewhere in this book.

Support of student independence

View of man
Social balance as basic principle: All men are dependent on support. The success of the individual is promoted through supporting institutions. Far-reaching support is regarded as a moral and social duty.

Central institutional characteristics
Teaching is regarded as support and facilitation of the learning of problem-solving skills in certain areas. Support is expected to be given to a considerable extent. It can occur both as an offer to be accepted or rejected and as a directive intervention towards prescribed goals.

Range of possible institutional forms

Frames within which possibilities are offered to search for and identify individual goals and ways of study with the support of tutors. Example: Empire State College		Essentially prescribed courses with possibilities for individual selection and continuous active support and counselling. Example: The Open University (UK)
high	independence	low
medium to low	control	high

Expectation of student independence

View of man

Autonomy as basic principle:
The integrity of the personal sphere
must be safeguarded.
Institutional interventions in the
form of unsolicited support can be regarded as intrusion into the privacy
of individual students.

Central institutional characteristics

Teaching is regarded as the transmission of knowledge and skills which can
then be used by the learner in any way
found desirable.
Study support is expected to be
offered in a limited way as an offer
students may or may not make use of
and thus as an additional element.

Range of possible institutional forms

Frames within which possible goals and ways for students´ choice are offered with orientation and support. Information rather than direction, several selection possibil-ities.	Essentially pre-scribed courses strict direction limited selection possibilities.
Example: so far not found	Example: Fernuni-versitat

high	independence	low
low	control	medium

After Lehner & Weingartz in Graff & Holmberg 1985

To what has been said about this the following
findings could be added. If in examination
requirements problem solving is considered important
beside factual learning, then more attention is
given to the interaction between students and the
supporting organisation (phi = .15; n = 185;
p < .05)(4), intervention when students seem to be
in danger of drop out tends to occur (phi = .17;
n = 185; p < .05), and learner ´friendliness` is
higher (rho = .15; n = 185; p < .05). This is to
be related to considerations about the possible
threat to students´ integrity that interventions by
the supporting organisations might be regarded as.

Student friendliness

It was found possible and particularly interesting to study the ´friendliness` of the teaching,
i.e. the adaptivity of the distance teaching to
students´ individual needs and wishes. Hypotheses
were developed to the effect that distance-teaching
institutions are regarded by the students as
´friendlier`

-if they provide counselling and other
types of student support and if counselling and individual tutoring is considered
important as well as if the student-
support services are more or less
constantly accessible

-if the distance-teaching institutions
initiate contacts with students who have
not been heard from (intervention in the
face of possible drop out)

-if the institutions allow students to
submit assignments whenever it suits them
(thus no prescribed deadlines for
submission)

-if the assignments are not only corrected
but commented on fully and individually;
and

-if the turn-round-time of the assignments,
i.e. the time from the student´s dispatch
of the assignment until its return with
the tutor´s comments, is short.

Statistically significant correlations relevant to

the concept of ´friendliness` could be established. Thus,

the tendency to initiate contacts with students who have not been heard from is greater

- -if the distance-teaching institution provides organised counselling and student-support service (phi = .19; p < .01) or

- -if the interaction between learner and tutor is regarded as important (phi = .19; p < .01).

If the interaction between learner and tutor is considered important

- -then mere correction of assignments is not considered enough (phi = .20; p = .005) and

- -then the comments of assignments tend to concentrate on the individual achievements of the student (phi = .19; p < .01).

If the distance-teaching institution is in the habit of contacting students who are not heard from

- -then the tendency to comment on individual achievements is greater (phi = .23; p < .005) and

- -there is a tendency to shorten the turn round-time of student assignments (phi = .24; p = .001).

The positive coefficients, i.e. the tendencies, correspond to expectations. The characteristics of friendliness can be related to success and failure if course completion is regarded as success and this is contrasted with no submission whatsoever of assignments. It was found that the percentage of successful learners (5) increases

- -when the distance-teaching institution initiates contacts with learners who are not heard from (phi = .18; n = 138; p < .05),

- -when mere correction of submission assignments is not considered satisfactory

$(phi = .20; \quad n = 138; \quad p = .05)$,

-when tutors´ comments on each asignment
are at least half a page or more long
$(phi = .15; \quad n = 138; \quad p = .06).(6)$

The percentage of students involved who submit no
assignment tends to decrease

-when the distance-teaching institution
initiates contact with learners who are
not heard from $(rho = -.16; \quad n = 120; \quad p < .05)$

-when the comments on assignments are more
comprehensive $(rho = -.21; \quad n = 120; \quad p < .01)$ and

-when comments are given on individual
achievements $(rho = -.27; \quad n = 120; \quad p < .01)$

-when mere correction of assignments is not
considered satisfactory $(rho = -.22; \quad n = 120; \quad p < .01)$

The correlations between on the one hand student
success and student failure and on the other hand
indices of ´friendliness` show that

-the percentage of successful students
increases with increasing ´friendliness`
$(rho = .13; \quad n = 138; \quad p = .10)(7)$

-the number of students enrolled who submit
no assignments decreases with increasing
´friendliness` $(rho = -.18; \quad n = 120; \quad p < .05)$

Some further correlations that may be of interest
should be mentioned:

In the cases when the organisation encourages
students to approach their tutor

-the ´friendliness` index is higher:
$rho = .28; \quad n = 198; \quad p = .001$

-counselling and student support is considered important:
$phi = 20; \quad n = 198; \quad p < .01$

-intervention when a student is not heard
from tends to occur:
phi = .16; n = 198; p < .05

-correction of assignments is accompanied
by explanatory comments:
phi = .22; n = 198; p < .01

-tutor comments on assignments tend to
cover half a page or more:
phi = .17; n = 198; p < .05

-comments tend to be individual:
phi = .32; n = 198; p < .001

-assignment results tend to influence
examination marks:
phi = -.21; n = 198; p < .01.

In the cases when students can approach tutors and
counsellors on the telephone

-the ´friendliness` index is higher
(rho = .27; n = 169; p < .01) (8)

-there is a tendency not to allow students
to submit assignments at any time that
suits them (phi = -.18; n = 169; p < .05)

-mere correction of assignments tends not
to be considered satisfactory (phi = .27;
n = 169; p < .001)

-the size of assignment comments tends to
be half a page or more (phi = .21;
n = 169; p < .01).

If a personal tutor-counsellor is assigned to each
student

-the ´friendliness` index is higher
rho = .28; n = 186; p < .01)

-the institution tends to initiate contacts
to students who have not been heard from
(phi = .21; n = 186; p < .01)

-the students tend to be allowed more flexibility as to periods for submission of
assignments (phi = .18; n = 186; p < .05)

-the turn-round-time for assignments tends to be shorter (phi = .19; n = 186; p = .01)

-the comments on assignments tend to be comprehensive (phi = .14; n = 186; P = .06)

-the percentage of successful students is higher (rho = .18; n = 125; p < .05).

If a distance-teaching institution makes use of study centres for face-to-face meetings

-the learner ´friendliness` tends to be small (rho = -.16; n = 201; p = .06) (9)

-students´ rights to submit assignments at any time that suits them is limited (phi = -.19; n = 201; p < .01)

-turn-round-time for assignments tends to be longer (phi = -.14; n = 201; p < .05).

A great number of further correlations have been established. Only the following should be added to those already accounted for.

When courses are offered at the university level, students´ freedom to submit assignments whenever it suits them tends to be smaller (phi = -.20; n = 197; p = .005). The same seems to apply to distance-teaching institutions offering recognised degrees, diplomas and other competencies (phi = -.38; n = 196; p < .001) as well as generally to distance-teaching institutions which are public bodies (phi = -.20; n = 200; p < .01). As opposed to this private institutions tend to offer their students flexibility in this respect (phi = .19; n = 200; p < .01). When the distance-teaching organisation is a department of a traditional school or university, the turn-round-time for assignments tends to be longer than in other cases (phi = -.15; n = 192; p < .05).

Distance education as innovation

The picture of distance education emerging from the replies given to the questionnaire agrees with the innovatory character of distance education as described in Chapter 4 above. However, the replies

do so to a different extent. It seems to be proper
to describe distance education as actually applied
as a continuum starting rather close to conventional
face-to-face teaching making use of print and other
media and extending to systematic and full
application of the peculiar characteristics of
distance education. Cf. the large-scale vs
small-scale dichotomy referred to in the preceding
chapters.

Distance-teaching institutions are more or less
aware of their innovative character. Some stress
innovation as an essential goal. Not unexpectedly
these tend to apply the principles agreeing with the
concept of learner ´friendliness` discussed. Thus,
for instance, they pay more attention to counselling
and student support than others and their
inclination to initiate contact with students who
are not heard from is higher than from other respondents (phi = .15; n = 203; p < .05).

The relevance of the data

The data of the questionnaire study emanate
from a sample of uncertain status. They undoubtedly
represent prevalent practices and attitudes, but it
is uncertain to what extent the statistical
tendencies can be regarded as representative of all
distance education in the 1980s. Some reservations
of importance have already been expressed.

The situation can be illuminated by a quotation
from the present author´s first report on the study:

> When in the Institute for Research into
> Distance Education of the FernUniversitat
> in West Germany a comparative study was
> begun we found that we had in our files no
> less than about 1500 addresses of
> organisations in some way connected with
> this kind of education (distance-teaching
> universities, conventional universities
> with some distance teaching, schools,
> associations, companies, governmental or
> religious bodies). Whether a majority of
> them really provide distance-education
> services themselves is uncertain and among
> those which do some seem to cater for only
> highly specialised studies and small
> target groups (like the staff of a
> company). Apart from the bodies thus
> known to us there are undoubtedly several
> universities and other organisations in

the world concerned with distance
education, some of them in the form of odd
projects which may develop into permanent
activities. This will make it clear that,
although we are making a thorough study of
data known to us, we cannot claim to give
an accurate, all-inclusive presentation of
the status of distance education today.

After some preliminary studies we
started our project by writing to all the
organisations known to us and asking them
to fill in a questionnaire we had
developed in six languages (English,
French, German, Polish, Russian and
Spanish). Many of the recipients were
known to us only by name, and of others we
knew that they were evidently only
marginally concerned with distance
education. Our questionnaire was
comprehensive and, among other things,
asked for statistical information of a
sensitive type. There were postal
problems (in developing countries) and
both ideological and bureaucratic
problems (in Socialist countries). From
the beginning we thus had to count with a
high wastage percentage both in the sense
that our questionnaire was unanswered and
in the sense that replies had nothing to
contribute. This proved a realistic
assumption. We received 290 replies, out
of which only 203 were of a kind to make
an evaluation useful. From the USA 37
replies were received, from the United
Kingdom 23, from Australia 22, Canada 16
and the Federal Republic of Germany 15.
Of the East Bloc countries only Poland
replied.

(Holmberg 1985b p.1)

While it thus seems hazardous to draw any definite
inferences about all distance-education practices
from the sample studied, the study evidently
indicates characteristics, attitudes and values of
importance.

Conclusions

What conclusions, if any, can under the circumstances that apply, be drawn from this comparative
study.

The first conclusion is evidently that for fact-finding purposes the study must be continued, that greater representativity must be attained and that more detailed information must be acquired. This continuation of the research has duly begun.

Other conclusions can be drawn when specific issues are studied. Some of those discussed in Chapters 1-6 receive illumination of relevance through the study.

Thus it is evident that student autonomy is a concern of importance to today's distance educators. There is something of a conflict between those who take this autonomy more or less for granted and those who either consciously support it or in any case regard it as a social duty to help students towards success. In most cases success is then taken to mean course completion at an acceptable level whereas more idiosyncratic goal conceptions are hardly recognised. Not unexpectedly the students given support of various kinds are more successful in this sense than those of whom autonomous study is expected from the beginning. It is quite clear that there are two ideologies represented among distance educators on this issue. On the one hand there are those above all respecting mature students' integrity, thus expecting or demanding a high degree of autonomy and leaving both goal decisions and the judgment of goal attainment to the students themselves, on the other hand those regarding support of students as a social duty and thus undertaking to occupy a position of guardianship in relation to the students.

As could be expected the latter group of distance educators adopt principles and practices that can be described as exponents of student friendliness to a higher degree than the former. However, this does not mean that they consistently allow students a great amount of flexibility as to pacing and submission of assignments. Sometimes this type of flexibility is hindered or wholly prevented by the control 'student-friendly' organisations exert in the interest of students.

The publicly funded distance-teaching organisations (like the universities teaching at a distance) tend to control their students more strictly and seem to pay less attention to the innovatory potentials of distance education than private bodies. On this point the positions taken to on the one hand student autonomy, on the other hand student friendliness are to some extent blurred, as shown under 'Distance education as innovation' above.

The evident, summarising conclusion is that distance education, although a unity within the framework defined in Chapter 1, reflects a number of different views of students and the conditions of learning and teaching. Just as approaches vary, the student bodies concerned are heterogeneous entities. Diversity is a quality that can safely be ascribed to modern distance education in spite of the fact that, as shown in Chapter 6, there are a number of pervasive themes that have engaged distance educators for a century by now. However, not only themes have been pervasive; so have a number of controversies. This situation must needs be reflected in attempts made to create a theory of distance education. Nevertheless it may prove possible to develop theories of organisation and theories of teaching and learning compatible with mutually rather divergent types of thinking and practice.

NOTES

1. Applying customary statistical terminology the coefficient of correlation between two ordinal scales is represented by rho (Spearman), a measure varying on a scale between $+ 1$ and $- 1$. A rho of $+ 1$ signifies a perfect, positive correlation, $- 1$ a perfect, negative correlation.

2. The symbol p denotes probability. The statement $p < .001$ indicates that the probability of the event occurring by <u>chance alone</u> is smaller than one in 1000, $p < .01$ that it is smaller than one in 100 etc.

3. Tested by the Kruskal-Wallis test.

4. The phi coefficient (for 2 x 2 tables) is used to describe the degree of relationship between two naturally dichotomous or for special reasons dichotomised variables. Significance, tested by Fisher´s exact (one-tailed) probability test, here means $p \leq .05$, i.e. that the probability of an event´s occurrence by chance equals or is smaller than five in one hundred.

5. For these relationships the percentage scores were dichotomised.

6. Not statistically significant.

7. Not statistically significant.

8. Beginning here p for two-tailed test.

9. Not statistically significant.

Chapter 8

STEPS ON THE PATH TOWARDS A THEORY OF DISTANCE
EDUCATION

Some theoretical approaches to distance education
are well known and deserve careful attention. To
these belong the contributions made by John Bååth
(1979), Manfred Delling (1971), Michael Moore (1973
and 1977), Hilary Perraton (1981), Otto Peters
(1973 and 1983), David Stewart (1981), Kevin Smith
(1983) and Charles Wedemeyer (1981), for example.
Cf. also Keegan 1983. Sometimes search for a ´theory
of distance education` is referred to. This is a
concern which is necessarily closely related to
educational theory generally, theory of information,
communication and innovation, to social commitment
and endeavours to develop independent thinking.
Much of the discussion in Faure´s monumental Unesco
report of 1972 is relevant in this context.
    Nevertheless, more special attempts to look
into the feasibility of a theory of teaching for
distance education as well as a description of what
could constitute a more comprehensive theory of
distance education are overdue. The following is
meant to serve as a starting-point for further
considerations and to contribute facts, views and
arguments for elaboration or contradiction in a way
to promote theoretical underpinnings of practice in
the field.

Introduction

    The search for a theory that can guide
practical work is a complicated endeavour. Epistemological concerns must be considered, descriptive
elements must be identified, explanatory and
predictive potentials looked into. This complicated
picture requires a progression in the presentation
that should be elucidated in advance. The presentation will be structured as follows.

As an introduction the theory concept will be analysed, the relevance of induction and deduction in our context briefly referred to and the testing of hypothetico-deductive hypotheses discussed. The following steps will then be taken. First, a basis for a theory of distance education will be constructed as a descriptive foundation ordering facts and ideas about distance education in a systematic way. Second, theory development for distance education will be discussed and attempted and, after a tentative development of hypotheses concerning the organisation of distance education, the preliminary theoretical considerations will be summed up in the form of a general view of distance education.

As theories of teaching rather than theories of learning can be predictive, the teaching concept and the teaching element of distance education are then looked into with a view to establishing relationships between the teaching and the outcomes of learning. Explanatory and predictive teaching theories are discussed and the possible content of a theory of teaching for distance education, its potentials and limitations are investigated.

After all these inevitable preliminaries a proposed teaching theory is worded, hypotheses based on statements derived from the theory are developed and shown to be testable. The relevance and possible usefulness of this theory are then discussed.

Finally the chapter is summed up by the descriptive ordering of ideas, the general view of distance education and the theory of teaching for distance education being brought together.

The meaning and potential value of theory

The theory concept is problematic. in scholarly literature theory is a term used to denote different concepts. It is frequently used to refer to any systematic ordering of ideas about the phenomena of a field of inquiry (Gage 1963, p.102) as, for instance, when reference is made to the theory of distance education. This (or simply the opposite of practice?) is also meant when chairs at, for instance, German universities are devoted to ´theory of education` (Theorie der Erziehung) or ´theory of the school` (Theorie der Schule). This vague use of the term theory can be rather confusing as in other scholarly contexts a theory represents a structure of reasoned explanations, for which intersubjective testability is a <u>sine qua non</u> (cf. Brezinka 1978, pp.116-117). A theory in this sense may be expressed as a set of hypotheses logically related to one another in explaining and predicting occurrences. The hypotheses are then of the types 'if A then B' or 'the more A the more/less B'. Empirical data can confirm, refute or leave unresolved hypotheses of this kind. The normal starting point is a so far unsolved problem, for instance that of the influence of varying frequencies of assignment submission in distance education. Relevant data are then traced, collected and evaluated to help to solve the problem. Whether or not research intended to contribute to the solution of a problem is based on a theory <u>expressis verbis</u> depends both on the type of problem and on the philosophy of the researcher concerned. It is perfectly possible to investigate a subject area without any formulated theory, with a view to finding the answers to one or more questions. Experiments on teaching specific contents by different methods and/or by means of different text-book approaches, different types of exercises, etc., may be - and have been - conducted without any explicit reference to a theory (but naturally based on the theories of the competing methods and the theoretical position that causes the research). If, for instance, we wish to know whether a certain curriculum content in a foreign language is learnt more effectively by an imitative method or by a cognitive method, this problem can be investigated without the backing of a theory indicating an expected answer. It is possible, but not necessary, to hypothesise that one or the other of the methods is the more effective of the two, or to assume that there is no difference, the so-called null hypothesis.

Whereas in the heyday of positivism and behaviourism it was considered acceptable to collect and evaluate data without any theoretical background, which, in fact, meant an inductive approach, it is now much more common to insist that a theory to guide this study and make deductions possible must be developed before any empirical investigation is made. In Popper's spirit induction has become something of a dirty word. Cf., however, Glaser & Strauss 1977 and Covill-Servo & Hein 1983, p.306.

What, then, is the logical background of this insistence on an explicit theory preceding an empirical investigation? Is is a consequence of a desire to define in advance what is worth while investigating and creating awareness in the scholar´s mind of what is reasonable to expect? Or is it largely - or in combination with the reasons referred to - an attempt to make the study deductive rather than inductive in character? Those adhering to Popper´s epistemological principles will insist that explanations require deductive theories.

I fear that in many cases in point here the distinction between induction and deduction is rather illusory. The knowledge of numerous instances of something happening, i.e. an inductive process, may cause the development of a theory from which are deduced possibly refutable hypotheses, which are then tried out empirically. This could, for instance, occur (and has occurred) after constantly recurring experiences of the learning-supporting influence of personal approaches in distance education.

The real problem here would seem to be whether the basic observations made by the researcher before the theory is worded have been consciously or sub-consciously structured by his expectations or general thinking. This would not then be a case of induction proper. Sometimes, however, it is doubtful if we have reason to postulate an implicit theory. This would seem to apply to the expected outcome of the study mentioned of two competing methods for language learning. This seems to be a school example of an inductive study unless, which has been done, a theory is provided from which a refutable answer is deduced. The empirical study made can be identical in the two cases, however.

In the background of this game there is a complicated philosophical problem concerning what Bertrand Russell calls the validity of inference, i.e. of induction in the sense of inferring general laws from particular instances: ´A very little consideration shows that, logically, the inference cannot be demonstrative, but must ·be at best probable. It is not logically impossible that my life may be one long dream... If we are to reject this view, we must do so on the basis of an inductive or analogical argument, which cannot give complete certainty´ (Russell 1951, p.278).

The powerful objections against the clear-cut positivist assumptions of the reliability of inductive conclusions that Popper and his school of ´critical rationalists´ have delivered would seem to make many scholars healthily wary of inductive methods (Popper 1980, pp.27-30, 254-265). The critical rationalists are no doubt right in insisting that theories cannot be proved, that we must accept permanent uncertainty, and that theories to be studied deductively must be empirically refutable rather than confirmable so that the non-refuted theory is simply considered to have a higher degree of verisimilitude than its competing counterpart. However, this does not fully do away with the seemingly artificial technical conversion of induction into deduction described as a game above.

The ´grounded-theory` method (Glaser & Strauss 1977) is interesting in this context. It implies theory development through inductive methods in that researchers are expected to collect and analyse data, beginning with observations of phenomena, and from there proceed to selection of what is relevant and to deriving a theoretical approach. As shown above this is undoubtedly how some theories gradually emerge. As the collection of data is necessarily selective and based on some kind of theoretical understanding it seems possible to query whether the Glaser & Strauss approach should be described as consistently inductive. To test theories developed in the way indicated Popperian method is in any case eminently suitable. The theories would then be both grounded in and tested by data.

To bring order and cohesion into the many-sided observations and occurrences that are studies in educational contexts is evidently of paramount importance. This endeavour gives a mighty stimulus to basing research aimed at understanding and/or explanation on a theoretical concept representing a structure of reasoned explanations.

The feasibility of a theory of distance education and a proposed basis

A theory explaining and predicting occurrences in distance education is imaginable as far as teaching and learning are concerned. Under 3 below an attempt to develop such a theory of teaching for distance education will be presented. However, any wider theory in the sense of ordering ideas about the phenomena of distance education requires a descriptive foundation raising problems open to theoretical considerations. Thus at the outset a series of characteristic points (explicitly and implicitly referred to in the preceding chapters and introduced in Chapter 1) should be considered. They seem relevant at least in the context of developed

Western societies and most probably largely apply
also to many developing societies.

1. Some basic statements

Succinctly the author´s thinking behind the
salient principles, characteristics and the practice
of distance education may be described as follows:

1.1 General principles

Learning is basically an individual process.
Cf. Sims 1977, p.18. Study support facilitating
this individual process is part and parcel of
education.
Individual learning can be supported non-
contiguously, i.e. without any face-to-face contact
between the student and the university or school
that organises distance education (here as a
translation of Delling´s ´helfende Organisation`
called the supporting organisation); this applies
particularly to mature students, the traditional
target group of distance education.
Study support requires on the one hand
presentation of facts and learning matter (one-way
traffic), on the other hand interaction between
students and the supporting organisation (tutors,
counsellors etc.), i.e. two-way communication.
Two-way communication serves counselling and
teaching, i.e. helping the student to learn, to
query, to discuss and to come to conclusions.
Learning and support of this learning organised
non-contiguously constitute distance education.
Protagonists of distance education often claim
that it has special potentials for promoting
students´ autonomy in carrying out the study and in
selecting study objectives and procedures; it is -
as shown above - undeniable that such possibilities
exist, but so far less than clear to what extent
they are applied.
The relative importance of one-way presentation
of learning matter vs interaction varies (cf. Moore
on distance as a function of dialogue and structure
referred to under 2 below).

1.2 Methods and media in distance education

1.2.1 Overriding considerations

Teaching is taken to mean facilitation of
learning (cf. Rogers 1969).

Teaching is to support motivation (and thus learning); it is propounded that this can best be achieved by engaging the student in considerations and decisions about the study, its objectives, contents and processes.

Feelings of belonging, personal relations and __rapport__ between the students and the supporting organisation are to be fostered by the methods and media applied as these feelings are assumed further to support study motivation and facilitate learning.

1.2.2 One-way traffic

Learning matter is presented by courses developed for distance education or by selected texts, the study of which is facilitated by specially prepared study guides. Various media are used to present learning matter. The by far most important medium is the printed word. Other media are, for example, audio and video recordings, live radio and TV broadcasts and computer presentation.

The pre-produced self-contained course or study guide is to facilitate access to what is to be read, listened to and watched as part of the learning.

A personal way of address and style of presentation inviting students to articulate their views is to characterise course materials prepared for distance education; in this way communication is simulated and students´ interaction with the course materials acquires something of the character of a didactic conversation (Holmberg, Schuemer & Obermeier 1982).

1.2.3 Two-way traffic

Interaction between students and the supporting organisation occurs regularly; this interaction can either be initiated by the latter, usually by assignments to be solved and submitted for correction and comment, or by students when encouraged to ask question, query arguments and comment on the course.

Various media can be used for this two-way traffic. The most important are the written word (correspondence) and telephone communication.

Simulated interaction as described under 1.2.2 supplemented by exercises for self-checking and comments on these is by some considered sufficient to meet the requirements for two-way traffic; this would seem to apply to the principles of most on-line types of computer- managed education, which limit interaction to that with a computer programme (by the use of computer terminals or micro-computers). In what is recognised as normal distance education here, interaction is live, however, i.e. there is communication between an individual student and an individual tutor (by correspondence, telephone conversations, computerised interaction and other types of person-to-person two- way communication).

1.3 Organisation

Organised distance education requires an administrative framework, within which processes are developed for the creation and distribution of learning materials, for counselling and interaction with students and for any other activity caused by the requirements of society in general and the educational establishment in particular (examinations, awarding of degrees, issue of certificates etc.). The university school or training institute in charge of this is in many respects a decision-making body, laying down policies, for instance those promoting student autonomy or those of strict control; it is identical with what Delling has called the supporting organisation.

The supporting organisation can be a public or private body, an independent institution or part of one, it can arrange examinations and award degrees or other formal competencies or can prepare students for examinations arranged by other bodies and/or can do entirely without preparations for examinations.

The structure, tasks and types of personnel of the supporting organisation depend on not only the distance-education activities per se but also on the societal contexts, the types of decision-making, finance and integration with other activities.

If large numbers of students are to be served, an industrial approach with division of labour, rationalisation and automation is practical and economical; cf. Peters 1973 and 1983. An author (Authors) with assisting staff or a course team, in which specific tasks are assigned to each member, can develop a course for hundreds or thousands of students, whereas a great many individual tutors each supervise and support a small number of these.

This approach tends particularly to stress the course development to which much attention is given.

Small-scale approaches on the other hand tend particularly to emphasise the personal interaction between students and tutors; each tutor may then develop his/her own, necessarily unsophisticated, course for a particular group of students and himself/herself supervise each student´s work (Smith 1983). Here the stress is on the interaction rather than on the pre-produced course.

The two approaches outlined require different types of organisation for course development, e.g. course teams, facilities for technical service, for recourse to external expertise etc. Cf. Holmberg 1983a.

2. Developing a theory

Michael Moore has developed a ´theory` of independent study, classifying educational programmes on the two dimensions of autonomy and distance which he describes in the following way:

> Autonomy is the extent to which the learner in an educational program is able to determine the selection of objectives, resources and evaluation procedures.......
> Distance in an educational program is a function of dialogue and structure. Structure is the extent to which the objectives, implementation procedures and evaluation procedures of the teaching program can be adapted to meet the specific objectives, implementation plans and evaluation methods of a particular student´s learning program. Dialogue is the extent to which interaction between learners and teacher is possible.........
> To the extend that a program "consists of pre-produced parts, at least in the form of particularized plans listing item by item the knowledge and skills to be covered by the Program" (1), the program may not be responsive to learners´ idio-syncracies, and structure is said to be high...................................
> ...when dialogue is difficult, or impossible, and when structure is high, "admonitory acts" become difficult or impossible. In a programmed text, such as Mager´s, a minimum of dialogue between

teacher and learner is obtained by use of the branching technique. The admonitary acts, such as "oops! You didn´t follow instructions", are weak by contrast to the power such statements would carry in a highly dialogic interaction. In tele-mathic teaching "directive action" is more easily communicated than admonition, but the teacher must assume that a large part of direction, as well as admonition, will be self-administered by the learner. The less distance, the more direction will be feasible. Even the most distant teachers are able to communicate "logical operations". Whether a particular learner will benefit from a program low in distance, or from a highly telemathic program is determined by the extent to which he benefits or is impaired by direction and admonition. This is determined by his competence as an autonomous, or "self-directed" learner.

(Moore 1977a, pp.33, 18 and 20)

The highest degree of distance occurs when a person studies without any support at all, which Moore describes as ´programs with no dialogue, and no structure` and examplifies by ´independent reading-study programs of the "self-directed" kind`. A normal distance-study course provides facilities for interaction (´dialogue`) as well as structure in Moore´s sense. Moore has made an empirical study of the hypothesis that autonomous persons are particularly attracted to distant methods of learning and teaching, which has been, on the whole, confirmed although it has also been found that distant students do not reject guidance (Moore 1976).

The two dimensions of autonomy and distance are relevant to various aspects of theory development for distance education.

If in a theory of distance education we wish to include not merely a systematic ordering of ideas behind a phenomenon, but a set of hypotheses logically related to one another in explaining and predicting occurrences, our search for a theory of distance education seems primarily to have to be directed towards the organisational frame-work and the facilitation of learning.

STEPS ON THE PATH TOWARDS A THEORY

2.1 Organising distance education

Regarding organisation at least the following three hypotheses are among those that more or less immediately present themselves:

o   The less dependent the study is of societal control and of prescribed curricula and procedures, the greater the possibilities both to individualise the work and to support student autonomy.

o   If industrialised working methods are used including systematic planning of courses, standardised procedures, mechanisation and division of labour, then the standard of pre-produced courses is likely to be high (although with limited possibilities for individualisation) and distance education will be particularly cost-effective for courses with large student numbers.

o   If a small-scale approach is applied including course creation by individual tutors, who also themselves teach students at a distance by interacting with them non-contiguously, then there is some likelihood that the study can to some extent be adapted to individual student needs and wishes whereas no cost advantages in comparison with conventional education are to be foreseen.

Other hypotheses related to the organisation of distance education are possible and plausible. They can, for example, concern

o   the factors leading to different types of organisations, for example goals, target groups, social and cultural frame factors

o   the educational and administrative conse-quences of organisational structures

o   effectiveness and economics.

The factual background of these and similar hypotheses is to be found in the basic characteristics of distance-education institutions and the interrelationships of these characteristics. Cf. Graff & Holmberg 1984, pp.10-11 and 37-57.

113

Hypotheses of the kinds indicated are evidently generated from theoretical considerations about what distance education is and should be, but so far it seems too early (in our field) to formulate a comprehensive, explanatory and predictive theory of organisation encompassing hypotheses logically related to one another. For the time being I limit myself, as far as organisation is concerned, to the following general view of distance education:

> Societal conditions and other frame factors influence distance education strongly. A supporting organisation administering distance education promotes student learning within the possibilities open to it. Various types of distance education are to be envisaged (large-scale, small-scale; training and preparations for degrees on the one hand and liberal education for personal enrichment on the other hand; autonomy-promoting study and study strictly planned and controlled, etc.). If not prevented by external control or prescribed curricula, it can offer highly individualised education. Industrial working methods can make it very cost-effective (large numbers of students being taught with one pre-produced course) and can, through a mass-communication approach, offer study opportunities to large numbers of people.

2.2 The nature of a theory of teaching

As indicated above it seems possible to go further in attempts to develop a theory of teaching and learning for distance education. With my understanding of teaching as facilitation of learning it appears admissible to couple these two concepts.

2.2.1 The teaching concept

It is quite common that both students and teachers regard ´knowledge as a commodity which can be transferred, by the act of teaching, from one container to another or from one location to another. Such people tend to express their view of teaching as "imparting knowledge" or "conveying information" (Fox 1973, p.152). There are several arguments against this rather primitive view of teaching, as made clear by Fox in the paper quoted. The main reason why I reject it is its implicit view of learners as passive receivers, which can under no circumstances be a true picture. I regard teaching as facilitation of learning meant to lead to a goal of some kind (self-realisation, an examination, professional competence or some other goal). This definition is important to rid us of the well-grounded objection that teaching and learning are sometimes little related to each other. It has rightly enough been said that when some-thing has been learnt in a teaching-learning situation, learning may have been caused by other influences than those of the teaching. When something has been taught we do not know whether something has been learnt, and, in fact, if something has been learnt we do not automatically know what; possibly something different from what was intended by the teaching has been learnt (cf. Loser & Terhart 1977, p.29).

Teaching is an attempt – and sometimes a successful attempt – to facilitate learning towards some goal.

2.2.2 Predictive teaching theories

It may be useful first to look at attempts made in relation to what can or should be expected of a deductive theory of teaching. It is common practice to expect of such theories that they should <u>inter alia</u>:

-have internal consistency as logical systems

-establish functional relationships between the teaching and the outcomes of learning

-be capable of generating specific hypotheses and predictions (cf. Snow 1973, pp. 104-105)

-be expressed in such a way that research data capable of possibly refuting (falsifying) them can be collected.

Bruner refers to four major requirements of a theory of instruction, namely:

1. specifying experiences effectively implanting ´in the individual a predisposition toward learning`;

2. defining ´optimal structure` conducive to ´simplifying information`, ´generating new propositions`, ´increasing the manipulability of a body of knowledge` and ´related to the status and gifts of the learner`;

3. specifying ´the most effective sequences in which to present the materials to be learned`;

4. specifying ´the nature and pacing` of extrinsic and intrinsic reinforcement (in Bruner´s terminology ´rewards and punishments`) (Bruner 1971, p.40).

Theories of teaching of this type are evidently predictive (as opposed to theories of learning which are descriptive in their attempts to explain how learning occurs). This understanding of the theory concept only partially agrees with Popper´s epistemological principles, according to which the task of scholarship is on the one hand theoretical, to bring about explanation, on the other hand practical, to provide for application or technology (Popper 1972, p.49). A predictive theory stresses the practical aspects, techniques and means more than explanation and thus does not meet Popper´s requirements. It is more in line with H.A. Simon´s type of normative theory, which ´rests on contingent propositions like: "If process X is to be efficacious for attaining goal Y, then it should have the properties A, B, C"` (Simon 1973, P.473).(2)
It would not seem to be very difficult to formulate a very general series of recommendations assumed to some extent to meet Bruner´s requirements. However, as soon as we try to be more specific the difficulties predominate over the possibilities. Each subject has its own character and within each subject there are several specialities. All these subject areas will have their own requirements. Thus, for instance, specifying the most effective sequences as required by Bruner is one thing in

a mathematical discipline and something quite different in a foreign language or in the social sciences. The prospect of listing all imaginable subject areas and for each of them specifying conditions in accordance with the requirements mentioned and co-ordinating these into a cohesive theory is intimidating, indeed. What is even worse, however, if a serious attempt is really made to create such a comprehensive theory of teaching, is the fact that human beings between them as well as their conditions of life and learning are so different that it is impossible to prescribe in any detail what the teaching should be like that could meet the requirements mentioned by Bruner.

There can be no doubt that a general theory of teaching of this kind applicable to all kinds of and all individual students as well as to all imaginable study areas and all frame factors is an impossibility. Hosford articulates this impossibility in two laws: '(1) It is necessarily impossible to determine the absolute value of any instructional procedure by any experiment whatsoever; (2) It is necessarily impossible to determine an absolute set of instructional procedures that will be "best", for different learners, or for different learnings by one learner` (Hosford 1973, pp.87 and 114).

If we attempt to develop a predictive theory of teaching we must be very modest. Education as a research area is, of course, concerned with human beings with personalities, hopes and wills of their own. If we are not determinists in the sense that we totally reject the assumption that human will is in any respect free, then it is impossible to postulate any automatic cause-effect principle in research aiming at optimising educational methods and procedures. Here theories usually have to be limited to statements to the effect that if such and such a measure is taken under specific circumstances, then this is likely to facilitate learning. This can be reworded into the semblance of a nomological theory, i.e. one that is always and under all circumstances applicable unless the validity is expressly limited to specific circumstances: if x, then conditions making y possible will be created. The situation is somewhat different in general

117

learning theory and other descriptive rather than prescriptive studies. It has been suggested that an agent´s decision-scheme, i.e. set of attitudes to reality, problems and solutions, dictates what he will do if he acts rationally: when A, then the rational action will be B (Lessnoff 1974, p.89 on Watkins´ ´imperfect rationality`).

This cautious conclusion is to be compared with Hosford´s appreciation of the influence of teaching. Starting out from his ´axiom` that ´change is the only absolute in education` he modestly claims that ´instructional events affect the pace and direction of change` (Hosford 1973, pp.87 and 114). Change here is deduced from the goal-orientation of teaching.

2.3 The possible content of a theory of teaching for distance education

My preliminary assumption is that distance teaching can, like Hosford´s general ´instructional events`, affect the pace and direction of learning. The content of a distance-study course, its general approach (for instance, authoritative statements of facts and ´correct` solutions of problems vs problem-orientation with discussions of possibilities and encouragement of students´ own contributions), the tuition provided (mainly correction or argumentative discussion of students´ suggestions) are doubtless decisive for the direction of learning. The pace of learning is influenced by such things as the readability of course materials, the frequency and turn-round time of submission assignments, the media used, etc.

It would not seem to be presumptuous to go a little further. No doubt the retention of what has been learnt can be influenced by teaching procedures applied to distance education (closeness to practice, methods and media, for instance the use of laboratory kits, exercises with comments, etc.). Further it goes without saying that the educational content of a pre-produced course is within the field of teaching influence in distance education. This is related to the view of teaching and learning embraced by course developers and tutors. Fox identifies four approaches or ´basic` "theories of teaching". There is the transfer theory which treats knowledge as a commodity to be transferred from one vessel to another. There is the shaping theory which treats teaching as a process of shaping or moulding students to a predetermined pattern. Thirdly, there is the travelling theory which treats a subject as a terrain to be explored with hills to be climbed for better viewpoints with the teacher as the travelling companion or expert guide. Finally, there is the growing theory which focuses more attention on intellectual and emotional development of the learner. These theories are reflected by, and interact with, the views that students have of the process of learning. Whichever theory a teacher uses to help him/her think about the process it will affect the strategies she/he uses and it will colour his/her attitudes to students and to any training programme that she/he undertakes' (Fox 1983, p.151).

Our view of what learning is influences teaching, which cannot but influence the learning outcome in some way. If course developers consider knowledge to be a ready-made product ('a commodity to be transferred') their courses will be rather different from those written by persons who favour problem-solving approaches. Monika Weingartz has, on the basis of a consistent view of learning as understanding and problem-solving, provided an in-depth analysis of some distance-study courses from different parts of the world illustrating these differences (Weingartz 1980 and 1981), and Helmut Lehner has developed a learning theory bearing on this. He describes all learning as problem-solving in the sense that it is composed of making assumptions (i.e. developing hypotheses) and modifying these as the learning progresses - an application of Popper's epistemological principle of 'conjectures and refutations'. This leads Lehner to what (like Wagenschein and others) he terms a 'genetic learning approach' (Lehner 1978 and 1979). Starting out from problems instead of from the comprehensive systems that the knowledge amassed through the centuries constitute (for instance, when studying gravitation asking the questions of Aristotle and Galileo in the way Einstein & Infeld do instead of starting by learning the solutions found) favours genetic learning (Lehner 1978, pp.76-77). Weingartz's theoretical approach is linked with Lehner's and has led her to study current practice in distance education. To judge from her study, much remains to be done to improve problem-solving learning in distance study, where on the whole the 'ready-made system' presentation dominates, although guidance in far-reaching problem solving occurs in some courses.

119

There can be no question of our universally preferring one type of learning or prescribing one of Fox´s types of teaching only. The target groups, the study objectives, the academic levels and similar considerations vary, and so must the teaching/learning approaches. Even those who accept Lehner´s learning theory, according to which learning is problem solving, will recognise the need for different procedures related to types of teaching and learning. In university study problem-solving approaches including critical use of sources and the application of Fox´s growing theory are usually appropriate. It is more questionable if they are applicable to, for example, a postman´s learning of lists of post offices along railway lines by heart (even though this is also a kind of problem solving according to Lehner, the problem being how best to commit the items to memory). Between these extremes there are vast numbers of teaching/learning situations with specific requirements.

These considerations (content, direction and pace of learning, retention, types of teaching and learning) and no doubt a great many others are relevant to any theory of teaching for distance education. When below - in agreement with my view of teaching as facilitation of learning - I refer to certain teaching factors as favourable to learning, the implication is that they are taken to favour the ease and speed of learning as well as its quality and retention.

2.4 Potentials and limitations of theories of teaching for distance education

As shown above it seems impossible to develop a theory of teaching universally applicable to all students, all conditions and all subject areas. It is very proper to give up the attempt to create theories of this kind. The question is if this means that we must also do without less exacting theories of teaching for distance education. It is certainly the safe approach as anyone trying to formulate any theory of this type lays himself/ herself open to easily motivated attacks. Per definitionem a crude theory attempt of the type possibly within reach must be very general and leave many considerations out of account. Nevertheless I will try to formulate a kind of theory generating hypotheses which seem to me generally relevant and decisive for teaching at a distance.

A general problem is if we can at all postulate cause-effect relationships when - as in distance education and all kinds of education - human beings are concerned. In my view this is not possible except as explained above in my reference to the semblance of a nomological theory. This means that a theory of teaching for distance education can include no other hypotheses than those stating that if teaching characterised in a particular way is applied, then this is likely to (or: will in most cases) facilitate learning.

A theory of distance education may be expected to indicate and explain the consequences of the various procedures and media applied to target groups of various kinds and to various frame factors. While, as apparent from the above, I regard it as impossible to develop a theory covering all imaginable cases of this kind, something can no doubt be done in this direction.

It is important to make clear what type or types of distance education a theory is focused on. Michael Moore's description of distance in an educational programme as a function of dialogue and structure` is relevant here. Cf. above, the beginning of Section 2 of this chapter.

A theoretical approach to distance education can start out from various points on the continuum indicated, for instance from a comparison with face-to-face teaching with its high degree of dialogue (cf. Peters 1973) and from systems making ample use of supplementary face-to-face sessions. My approach will be from the other end of the continuum, investigating ´pure` distance education, i.e. teaching exclusively at a distance, which is in any case the basis of distance education. My questions are:

1. What basic characteristics distinguishing it from self-directed learning should distance teaching have to be able effectively to help students to learn?

2. What procedures and measures make pre-produced courses and non-contiguous communication effective as teaching instruments?

3. Why are the basic characteristics and methods chosen effective?

3. A suggested theory of teaching for distance education

Against this background and with the reservations mentioned in mind I describe my theory of teaching for distance education like this:

General background assumptions are

o   that the core of teaching is interaction between the teaching and learning parties; it is assumed that simulated interaction through subject-matter presentation in pre-produced courses can take over part of the interaction by causing students to consider different views, approaches and solutions and generally interact with a course

o   that emotional involvement in the study and feelings of personal relation between the teaching and learning parties are likely to contribute to learning pleasure

o   that learning pleasure supports student motivation

o   that participation in decision-making concerning the study is favourable to student motivation

o   that strong student motivation facilitates learning

o   that a friendly, personal tone and easy access to the subject matter contribute to learning pleasure, support student motivation and thus facilitate learning from the presentations of pre-produced courses, i.e. from teaching in the form of one-way traffic simulating interaction, as well as from didactic communication in the form of two-way traffic between the teaching and learning parties

o   that the effectiveness of teaching is demonstrated by students´ learning of what has been taught.

The first six of these assumptions, though used deductively, could be described as being based on inductive observations. The uncertain distinction between deduction and induction discussed above would seem to apply. Whatever their provenance, the assumptions constitute the basis of what I consider to be essential teaching principles for distance education. Thus I formulate my normative teaching theory as follows:

> Distance teaching will support student motivation, promote learning pleasure and effectiveness if offered in a way felt to make the study relevant to the individual learner and his/her needs, creating feelings of rapport between the learner and the distance-education institution (its tutors, counsellors etc.), facilitating access to course content, engaging the learner in activities, discussions and decisions and generally catering for helpful real and simulated communication to and from the learner.

This general theory of mine seems to have explanatory value in relating teaching effectiveness to the impact of feelings of belonging and cooperation as well as to the actual exchange of questions, answers and arguments in mediated communications. It is a communication theory which causes me to identify as favourable to teaching, i.e. facilitation of learning:

1. a presentation of course goals or objectives engaging the student in the evaluation of their relevance and, if at all possible, in their selection

2. a course structure carefully based on required earlier learning making sub-sumptions in Ausubel´s sense (3) possible and more or less a matter of course

3. pre-produced course materials characterised by a conversational style with invitations to an exchange of views and with attempts to involve the student emotionally

4. a style of presentation that is easily accessible; a high degree of readability of printed course materials

5. graphical and typographical presentations

> facilitating access to printed courses and selection of relevant subject matters

6. a choice of media, sequencing and other principles for course presentation adapted to student needs and to the requirements of subject areas studied, e.g. those of <u>operations on knowledge</u> and <u>operations with knowledge</u> (Chang et al 1983, pp.14-16)

7. communication facilities (in writing, on the telephone and/or by audio tape) constantly open to students for questions and exchanges of opinions with tutors and counsellors

8. frequent submission of assignments requiring students to solve problems, evaluate texts or recordings

9. friendly, helpful and extensive tutor comments on assignments submitted with suggestions expressed in a way to promote personal rapport between student and tutor; the same approach should characterise computer-marked and computer-commented assignments

10. quick handling of assignments

11. self-checking exercises in pre-produced courses through which students are induced to practice skills; not only model answers should be provided, but also extensive comments based on course writers´ experience of likely errors and misunderstandings.

It would, of course, be possible to specify each of these statements in more detail (for instance a plan for discussion contributions to be compared with the course writer´s suggestions in the seventh and ninth statements). I have limited my statements to those above as they seem to be fairly universally acceptable (even though they may not be really accepted). Others might like to add supplementary face-to-face sessions to the requirements derived from the wording of the theory, and personally I think students´ individual pacing with the right to submit assignments at any time (regardless of prescribed or suggested timetables) would be favourable. I consciously omit these and other controversial characteristics which could, but need not, belong to the statements specifying the theory.

While this is admittedly a leaky theory, does it meet the requirements specified above under 2.2.2 ´Predictive teaching theories`? I think so. It is true that it is not - and cannot be - nomological, i.e. deterministic; its background can, in spite of its deductive form, be interpreted as inductive; and it no doubt has too much of an instrumentalist character to meet Popperian requirements - all reservations discussed above - as it is a normative theory. However, it is not devoid of explanatory power: it does, in fact, indicate essential characteristics of effective distance education. It would seem to be logically consistent and it does establish functional relationships between teaching and expected outcomes of learning. As to the requirements that it should be capable of generating hypotheses and predictions and be expressed in such a way that research data capable of possibly falsifying the theory can be collected, let us look at each statement in turn:

ad 1) An empirical study of alternative presentations of goals/objectives, one simply prescribing them, the other inviting students to discuss their relevance and, possibly, to influence their selection, could be made by providing two groups of students, selected at random among students of equal standard, with alternative versions. The attitudes of the students could be measured immediately after the presentation of objectives and after course completion; then course completion and achievement levels could also be compared. The hypothesis could be worded like this:

-If students are engaged in the evaluation of the relevance of suggested study objectives (and/or are given the opportunity to influence their selection), then their attitudes to the study will be more favourable and their achievements will be better than if objectives are simply prescribed (The more..., the better...).

It would also be possible to test similar hypotheses based on the more radical suggestions for student autonomy made by Ljoså & Sandvold 1976.

ad 2) A reference to Ausubel´s studies here should

be sufficient.

ad 3) This statement has been empirically studied - and given some statistical support - on the basis of four hypotheses:

-The stronger the characteristics of guided didactic conversation, the stronger the students' feelings of personal relationship between them and the supporting organisation.

-The stronger the students' feelings that the supporting organisation is interested in making the study matter personally relevant to them, the greater their personal involvement.

-The stronger the students' feelings of personal relations to the supporting organisation and of being personally involved with the study matter, the stronger the motivation and the more effective the learning.

-The more independent and scholarly experienced the students, the less relevant the characteristics of guided didactic conversation.

(Holmberg, Schuemer & Obermeier 1982)

ad 4) The relevant hypotheses here would be:

-The more easily accessible the pre-produced course, (the more readable the texts), the better the outcome of learning.

Among studies of this kind, necessarily operationalising the readability concept to make its influence testable, should be mentioned Langer, Schulz von Thun & Tausch 1974.

ad 5) It would be possible to operationalise Waller's concept of access structure (Waller 1977a and b) and test the hypothesis that

-if access-structure measures such as headlines, graphics and other typographical means are applied, then the learning outcome is improved in relation to the study of the same text without this access structure.

An empirical study could easily be arranged comparing two matched groups. Doerfert 1980 has studied this problem theoretically and empirically from the points of view of distance education.

ad 6) Hypotheses for individual principles, media and target groups can be formulated and tested empirically; this is the weakest of the eleven statements as in itself it implies no prediction, but merely indicates that predictions may be tested by empirical studies of individual principles or media under specific circumstances.

ad 7) The hypothesis that

-if communication facilities of the kind described are provided, students will be more motivated and more successful than if left to themselves

could easily be tested, but seems to be too generally accepted among those concerned with helping students and too little interesting to those satisfied with information dissemination to have made anybody undertake this study.

ad 8) John Bååth's empirical investigation of this subject implied testing eleven hypotheses concerning differences caused by varying degrees of submission frequency with regard to study perseverance, attitudes, achievements and study time (Bååth 1980).

ad 9) The hypotheses here would be:

-If tutor comments are expressed in a personal style and are ostensibly based on a wish to be helpful (a matter of formulation), the students will be more satisfied with their study and the learning outcomes will be better than if the tutor comments consist of factual statements only.

This hypothesis is evidently empirically testable.

ad 10) This statement has been empirically tested - and has been given remarkably strong research support (Rekkedal 1983).

ad 11) It would be feasible to test the hypothesis that

-if a course contains self-checking exercises of the type mentioned, its students will be more successful than matching students taking the same course without these exercises.

An empirical study by Bååth of the possibility of replacing considerable numbers of submission assignments by self-checking exercises seems to indicate that exercises of the latter type with model answers and comments have no small potentials (Bååth 1980, p.152)

The claim that the hypotheses generated are testable and that data capable of possibly falsifying the theory can be collected would thus seem to be well founded.

4.   What requirements does the theory attempt provided meet?

What can be expected of a theory of distance education is expressed well by Desmond Keegan:

A firmly based theory of distance education will be one which can provide the touchstone against which decisions - political, financial, educational, social - when they have to be taken, can be taken with confidence. This would replace the ad hoc response to a set of conditions that arises in some ´crisis` situation of problem solving, which normally characterise this field of education.

(Keegan 1983, p.3)

While the preliminary general theory fragment introduced above (under 1 and 2.1) is by no means such a decisive touchstone as desired, it does indicate what the use and fields of activity of

distance education can be within different societal
and educational contexts. The 'touchstones' are
concepts like individualisation, industrialisation,
student autonomy, motivation, rapport between
students and their supporting organisation,
facilitation of access to learning and didactic
conversation.

The presentation of what facilitates learning
in distance education (3 above) is more specific.
It can - if the criteria listed above in concurrence
with Bruner, Simon, Snow and others are accepted -
be called a theory. With my definition of teaching
it is a theory of teaching. As such, has it
anything to convey or is it, because of its openness
and lack of detailed prescriptions for every
possible situation, merely an empty truism?

If a truism, the theory of teaching for
distance education would be universally accepted.
It is most unlikely that this should be the case.
In common practice there is implicit evidence to the
contrary. Many courses for distance education are
developed in a handbook style entirely contrary to
statements 1 and 3. It is exceptional rather than
the rule that a participative approach as presented
in statement 1 is applied. Some distance-education
organisations pay little attention to the
accessibility of their courses, whether readability
is meant as in statement 4 or typographical
facilitation is meant as in statement 5. Also
statement 6, in spite of its meagre content,
prescribes principles frequently not adhered to.
The medium or media are rarely chosen on the basis
of students' needs and more often in relation to
tradition or availability (e.g. TV time to be shared
between faculties and subjects).

Even greater deviations from the theory are
apparent when the communication aspect is
considered. Many distance educators pay scant
attention to (and many probably do not recognise)
the requirements of statements 7 and 8, whereas lip-
service is often paid to statement 9. Statement 10
clearly differs both from prevalent theory and
practice (in spite of remarkably univocal research
support!), whereas statement 11 is probably more in
accordance with common notions and practice than the
other statements.

It is uncertain to what extent statement 2 with
its adherence to Ausubel is usually accepted.
Nominally the identification of entrance
qualifications may be interpreted as acceptance, but
may also be nothing but a concession to the

requirements of formal educational systems.

The theory suggested is apparently not entirely devoid of content although - and this must be admitted without any reservation - it does not offer solutions to very specific teaching problems in distance education. It does not prescribe steps to be taken in the teaching of individual subjects at specified levels or with special types of students and it contains no taxonomy for media selection or structuring measures. What does it contribute then?

The proposed theory of teaching has some explanatory power as it provides an applicable general outline of effective teaching in distance education. It identifies suitable initial behaviour (student participation in goal considerations, sub-sumption under existing cognitive structures), it prescribes essential pervasive characteristics of course materials implying clear recommendations for course-development work, and it specifies require-ments for mediated communication, all relying on personal approaches.

As already mentioned (p.55 above) it indicates similarities between good distance education and conversations in a teaching situation. The pre-produced distance-teaching course on the one hand, the communication between students and their supporting organisation (tutors, counsellors) on the other hand are the instruments by means of which a conversation-like interaction is brought about. In the pre-produced course, which addresses the students in a personal way, activates them, makes them consider and come to conclusions of their own, the interaction is simulated. Real interaction occurs through communication in writing, by telephone etc. This theory was to some extent supported by empirical testing (Holmberg, Schuemer & Obermeier 1982). It is my contention that this theoretical approach together with the theory of teaching for distance education attempted above has something to say about the general character of well-functioning distance education, its ethos and underlying philosophy.

What is new in my presentation is the wording of a theory which generates testable - and, to some extent, even tested - hypotheses of the types ´If A, then B` and ´The more (less) A, the more (less) B`. However, much of the theoretical approach developed above on the basis of a description and an under-standing of the distance-education concept has a good deal in common with other presentations, for instance Delling´s and Perraton´s.

To Delling distance study is ´a multi-
dimensional system of learning processes in the
Distance Student, in the Helping Organisation, and
in the Society, and of communication processes among
the three by means of artificial signal carriers, in
particular as two-way communication between the
Distance Student and the Helping Organisation`
(Delling 1985b, p.4).

Perraton 1981, basing his arguments on a view
of education as connected with power and a case both
for expanding education as an egalitarian requirement and for stressing the importance of dialogue,
makes his contribution to a theory of distance
education in the form of fourteen hypotheses or
statements.

The dependence on political contexts is
stressed by Perraton. So are the possibilities
inherent in distance education for economies of
scale and the expansion of education, as evident
from his statements:

No 2: Distance teaching can break the integuments
of fixed staffing ratios which limited the
expansion of education when teacher and
student had to be in the same place at the
same time;

No 3: There are circumstances under which distance
teaching can be cheaper than orthodox
education, whether measured in terms of
audience reached or of learning; and

No 5: Distance teaching can reach audiences who
would not be reached by orthodox means.

Of special relevance in relation to my approach
are Perraton´s statements:

No 6: It is possible to organise distance teaching
in such a way that there is dialogue;

No 10: A multi-media programme is likely to be more
effective than one which relies on a single
medium;

No 11: A systems approach is helpful in planning
distance education;

No 12: Feedback is a necessary part of a distance-
learning system;

No 13: To be effective, distance-teaching materials should ensure that students undertake frequent and regular activities over and above reading, watching or listening.

Perraton finishes his theory paper by asking if his formulation of hypotheses suggests ´ways of testing them which would yield useful knowledge for practical educators` (p.24). This is, of course, exactly the concern which has caused me to develop my attempt at ´a theory of distance education` on the one hand as a descriptive and interpreting presentation, on the other hand, as far as this has seemed possible, as a set of hypotheses logically related to one another in explaining and predicting occurrences in distance education.

5 Summing up

My ´basic statements` under 1 above combined with the ´general view of distance education` presented under 2.1 constitute the basis of the theoretical approach suggested. An elaboration on teaching and learning in the form of an explanatory theory of distance teaching generating testable hypotheses (3 above) gives substance to this approach. This theory evidently establishes functional relationships between teaching and expected outcomes of learning. Together with the ´basic statements` and the ´general view of distance education` it indicates essential characteristics of distance education.

As shown above much is to be added. Systematic comparative analyses of empirical data may contribute to theory development. ´In order to discover basic conceptual elements to build into a theory we have to compare similar and dissimilar situations or events` (Moore 1985 commenting on the Glaser & Strauss ´grounded theory`). Comprehensive comparative studies are, in fact, under way as shown in Chapter 7. It is to be hoped that such studies of distance education and further theoretical considerations will contribute results of a kind to give to distance educators a firmly based theory, a touchstone against which decisions can be taken with confidence.

NOTES

1. A reference to Holmberg 1969, p.60.
2. According to Popper the aim of the theoretician ´is to find <u>explanatory theories</u> (if possible, <u>true</u> explanatory theories); that is to say, theories which describe certain structural properties of the world, and which permit us to deduce, with the help of initial conditions, the effects to be explained. ... My explanation of explanation has been adopted by certain positivists or "instrumentalists" who saw in it an attempt to explain it away - as the assertion that explanatory theories are <u>nothing but</u> premises for deducing predictions. I therefore wish to make it quite clear that I consider the theorist´s interest in <u>explanation</u> - that is, in discovering explanatory theories - as irreducible to the practical technological interest in the deduction of predictions. The theorist´s interest in <u>predictions</u>, on the other hand, is explicable as due to his interest in the problem whether his theories are true; or in other words, as due to his interest in testing his theories - in trying to find out whether they cannot be shown to be false` (Popper 1980, p.61).
3. Cf. Ausubel´s guiding principle: ´If I had to reduce all of educational psychology to just one principle, I would say this: The most important single factor influencing learning is what the learner already knows. Ascertain this and teach him accordingly` (Ausubel 1968 before the Preface).
4. For a detailed report (in German) on this theory and the testing of it see Holmberg, Schuemer & Obermeier 1982. The report is summarised in English in Sewart, Keegan & Holmberg 1983, pp.114-122.

Chapter 9

THE DISCIPLINE OF DISTANCE EDUCATION

Not along ago complaints about the lack of research into and serious writings about distance education were of frequent occurrence. A classical exponent of this is Child´s plea in 1969 that ´someone would perform a very great service indeed if he would undertake in a very serious and thoughtful way to relate the generally accepted principles of learning to the process of teaching by correspondence study´ (Childs 1971, p.118). As late as 1979 Baath, who took up Childs´ challenge (1), rightly states that ´on the whole there have been few attempts at systematically relating correspondence education to contemporary educational theories, models or approaches´ (Baath 1979, p.7). Omissions concerning other aspects of distance education were referred to by others. More or less at the same time an attempt was made to identify distance education as a new discipline, however (Holmberg 1978). Complaints concerning lacking documentation about distant students and about what really occurs in distance education continued for several years and are occasionally echoed even in the middle of the 1980s.

Distance education as the object of scholarly study

The fact is, however, that by the beginning of the 1980s the previous dearth of research had been replaced by a wealth of studies. When, in 1982, the present author prepared a research survey for the International Council for Distance Education, more than 300 studies of immediate and current relevance to distance education could be listed (Holmberg 1982b). Most of them had been published in the latter half of the 1970s and the beginning of the 1980s.(2) The research activities were and are geographically widely spread and a number of diverse areas are being investigated within the framework of distance education.

Some are concerned exclusively with didactics and methodology, some with cognition psychology etc., whereas others pay special attention to socio-logical topics and so on. It is evident that the study of distance education is benefiting from know-ledge and theory developed in disciplines estab-lished earlier and that most of the research done on distance education could be ascribed to these, for example to general education, pedagogics and andragogics, philosophy, psychology, sociology, history and economics.

When studies of these diverse types concentrate on the concerns of distance education and when they emerge as consequences of a desire to do basic and applied research, on as well as to attain expertise in, distance education, it is possible to describe these united efforts as the beginnings of a new discipline, that of distance education. This is so when distance educators on the one hand test the applicability of existing knowledge to their particular type of education and their target groups, on the other hand discover new knowledge and `new relationships within existing knowledge` (Jensen, Liveright & Hallenbeck 1964 [on adult education]). An additional criterion could be the teaching of the emerging discipline as a separate university subject.

Distance education as an emerging discipline

It would seem to be necessary when describing an emerging discipline to identify the scope and limitations of the search for knowledge and the teaching with which it is concerned. A sensible approach would then be both to make some sort of classification of its research and to list the subject areas included in curricula for the teaching of the new discipline.

Research

In the research survey of 1982 I identified fifteen areas on which serious studies had been published. These areas are:

1. General analyses of distance educa-tion, philosophy and theory

2. Studies of student bodies and

students´ motivation

3. Course planning and study objectives

4. Course development

5. Media

6. Non-contiguous tutorial two-way communication

7. Face-to-face sessions

8. Counselling

9. Institutional planning, organisation and administration

10. Economics of distance education

11. Evaluation

12. History of distance education

13. Distance education in developing countries

14. Guidelines for distance educators

15. Research on research

On the one hand each of these areas can include and also, to some extent at least, includes rather diverse research interests. Course development can be taken as an example. It includes text learning from the points of view of cognition psychology, readability, information theory, course structure, concept mapping, ´relational glossary` (Zimmer), so-called mathemagenic questions, self-contained courses vs study guides, graphic communication, questions of style in printed and recorded courses, organisation etc.

On the other hand the areas listed can be - and usually are - brought together into more comprehensive logical units. The Institute for Research into Distance Education (ZIFF) of the German FernUniversität has defined its overriding goal as describing, explaining and contributing to optimising distance education and works towards this goal by research (and development work) in three areas, viz:

o   target-group studies

o   investigations of the facilitation of learning by methods and media

o   systems research.

The first of these includes the following of the areas numbered above: 2, part of 3 (motivation), 8, parts of 9, 10, 11, 12 and 13; the second includes areas 1 (partly), 3, 4, 5, 6, 7, parts of 9, 10, 11, 12, 13 and 14; and the third includes 1, 15 and parts of the other areas listed.(3) Undoubtedly numerous other wide classifications of distance-education research can be found.

Against both this factual background and the presentation of the constituent elements of distance education, the pervasive arguments in its history and the problems discussed in the preceding chapters, the following reasonably articulated structure of the discipline of distance education would seem to emerge:

o   Philosophy and theory

o   Distant students, their milieu, conditions and study motivation

o   Subject-matter presentation

o   Communication and interaction between students and their supporting organisation (tutors, counsellors, administrators, other students)

o   Administration and organisation

o   Economics

o   Systems (comparative distance education, typologies, evaluation etc.)

o   History of distance education.

Educational, psychological, sociological, organisational, economic and other approaches are foreseen and have been applied to these various areas of research. The core is the understanding of distance education and the explanation of its processes and results. Various social and personal frame factors have to be considered as background variables. The explanatory task may lead to research-based development work.

Curricula for teaching distance education

Several years ago training of distance educators began to be offered in the form of face-to-face courses, mainly for third-world participants, by bodies engaged in work for development the German Foundation for International Development, Bonn, the International Extension College, London, SIDA, the Swedish authority for work in developing countries etc., and by some universities and other organisations (the University of Wisconsin, the International Council for Distance Education). Teaching distance education at a distance is a fairly recent phenomenon, which is in this context of particular interest as, like all distance teaching, its curricula, course materials, types of communication and other procedures are entirely open to scrutiny. For this reason three distance-teaching courses on distance teaching made available in the 1980s will be briefly presented here. They have been developed at and are being offered, primarily as post-graduate programmes, by the FernUniversitat in West Germany (FeU) (Baath 1984c, Holmberg 1982a), the Open Learning Institute of British Columbia, Canada (OLI) (Kaufman 1984) and the South Australian College of Advanced Education (SACAE) (Willmott & King 1984).

There seem to be some difference in the philosophical bases of the three courses, the SACAE one evidently, as opposed to the other two, challenging ´the heavily instrumental approach of distance educators` claiming to take an illuminative approach in the spirit of Parlett & Hamilton (Willmot & King 1984, pp.117, 119 and 120). Issues of principle related to this teaching were discussed in the journal Distance Education in 1984 (Willmot & King 1984 and Holmberg 1984). Whereas the OLI course makes use of various media (cf. Kaufman 1984, pp.249-250) and the SACAE one includes audio-taped components (Willmott & King 1984, p.123), the FeU course is entirely based on print and communication in writing.

In spite of these and other differences of approach the content of the three courses as illuminating the views held of the discipline shows great similarity. The concept, theory, rationale, and philosophy of distance education, the distant students, study motivation, course planning and course development (instructional design), self-checking exercises, communication and support strategies, media, organisation and administration, economics and evaluation of distance education are key elements in all three courses. Different degrees of attention are paid to the various elements mentioned and to subject areas like the history of distance education, information technology and general concerns of adult education, but there can be no doubt that behind the courses there is an implicit common view of what constitutes the discipline of distance education. This view agrees well with the one emerging from research done in the field, as shown above.

Distance education – an established discipline

From what has been said it is evident that there is in fact a discipline of distance education. It can be described both in terms of research programmes and in terms of curricula for university study.

While basically an educational discipline it includes aspects not only of closely related disciplines like philosophy, psychology and sociology, but also of history, economics and organisational theory. In part it could be regarded as a special kind of adult education, but as in educational practice it is applied also to children and youngsters, an application that has been the object of scholarly study (see the end of Chapter 2), distance education cannot properly be subsumed under this designation.

Whatever its relations to other subject areas distance education has de facto been established as a discipline for research and university study. The departments for research and development work in the distance-teaching universities and the so-called dual-mode institutions in various parts of the world, their documented work, the rich scholarly literature available and the occurrence of distance education as a university subject in which courses are offered are the tangible signs of the existence of this new discipline.

NOTES

1. Bååth made a systematic search to illuminate the relation of distance education to various current learning and teaching theories, among them Skinner´s behaviour-control model, Rothkopf´s model for written instruction, Ausubel´s advance organiser model, the model of Structural Communication, Bruner´s discovery-learning model, Rogers´ model for facilitation of learning, Gagné´s general teaching model. For each of them Bååth investigated its general applicability to distance study, the implications for the development of course material, for non-contiguous two-way communication, and for the supplementing of this two-way communication by face-to-face contacts. Further, he analysed some special relations between these various models and distance study. (Bååth 1979).

2. As early as 1971 Mathieson had published a list of no less than 170 contributions to the subject.

3. A presentation of this ZIFF research up to 1983 with a bibliography of reports was published in ´Higher Education in Europe` VIII, 3 (Holmberg 1983b).

Chapter 10

THE STATE OF DISTANCE EDUCATION TODAY

The picture of distance education emerging from the findings discussed in the preceding chapters has both clear contours and blurred patches. The following would seem to be a reasonable summary;

Distance education today is the product of a continuous development that started well over a century ago.

The overall characteristic of today´s distance education is that it is based on <u>non-contiguous communication</u>, which, however, does not exclude supplementary face-to-face sessions. The non-contiguous communication is brought about by on one hand a <u>pre-produced course</u>, as far as possible of a self-instructional character, in most cases basically in printed form although other media are also used, on the other hand systematic <u>two-way communication between students and tutors and other representatives of the supporting organisation</u>, i.e. school or university that arranges the distance-study facilities. For this communication the written word is the most commonly used medium; telephone communication is becoming more and more important, however, and so is computerised feed-back.

Whereas two-way communication (with the reservations voiced in Chapter 1) is a constitutive element of distance education, it is theoretically possible to do without a preproduced course, on condition that tutors in personal communications refer students to texts to be studied and provide individual tutorials, usually at a distance, i.e. mainly in writing, on the basis of these.

With the exception of supervised correspondence study and some support courses for grammar-school pupils distance education is almost exclusively a form of teaching and learning for <u>adults</u>. Those who make use of it are a far from homogeneous group. People choose distance study either because they <u>cannot</u> go to classes (because of distances, lack of a suitable course offer, irregular work hours, illness etc.) or because they <u>do not want</u> to do so. The reasons why people do not want to go to classes vary: some consider their study an entirely private matter, feel disturbed by the presence of fellow-students and want to study at odd hours that suit them, others regard the convenience of study at home as the most important thing. A special application is occupational further training financed by employers wishing to combine training with as far as possible uninterrupted work for the enterprise concerned. The possibility open to distant students to study in their spare time while continuing work has made distance education economically attractive.

The <u>economics</u> of distance education is strongly influenced by its potentials for <u>mass education</u> and what has been called <u>industrial working methods</u> (with large course editions, automation, rational-ising procedures and division of labour).

Whatever the procedure applied, distance education above all serves <u>the individual learner</u> who in principle studies when and where it suits him or her. Catering for largely autonomous study is possible and has been a prime concern in distance education since its inception.

Distance-study courses are, as a rule, prepared for use by large numbers of students. They are thus based on goal conceptions assumed to meet the demands of many unknown people. Any course with pre-specified objectives and contents runs the risk of presenting the students with ready-made solutions and what may be conceived of as definite truths, thus making the students passive receivers. This can hardly support autonomous thinking and may even exert negative influence on students´ independence.

To counteract these dangers inherent in distance study various measures occur. An argumentative presentation causing students to consider arguments for and against theories and statements is one. This is what has been called the <u>simulated didactic conversation</u>. Another is the use of modular courses allowing students to select the modules they want. A third possibility is to include in the course a selection of texts representing diverging views and approaches. Interaction with tutors - and even fellow-students - can further support pluralism.

For this and other purposes methods and media for the teaching-learning processes and for counselling have been developed. They include the use of information technology.

Various types of distance education occur, based on different needs, possibilities and philosophical principles. A lively discussion is being carried on aiming at identifying a theory of distance education as a touchstone for decisions. Apart from summaries of this discussion contributions are made in Chapter 8 of this book in the form of

o descriptive and characterising ´basic statements`

o a ´general view of distance education` bearing on its organisation

o a theory of teaching for distance education generating testable (falsifiable) hypotheses.

A number of principles of relevance to practice have constituted controversial issues among distance educators since the end of the nineteenth century. They are largely based on value judgments related to the rationale of distance education and, to some extent overlappingly, concern the degrees of individualisation and student autonomy to be aimed at, views of drop out and reactions to threatening course interruption, student integrity vs unsolicited student support, the character of course objectives and course presentations, the types of communication to be applied, organisational matters etc.

The author regards distance education not only as a vehicle for distributing knowledge matter but as a type of education in its own right. This view is supported by the finding that distance education has de facto been established as an academic discipline through research and university curricula.

Distance education has undergone an evolutionary process, which is illuminated by the fact that the concerns of the pioneers are still largely relevant both to theoretical considerations and to educational and administrative practice.

Towards the end of the 1980s a tendency to use what has so far been considered distance-study

procedures in on-campus university study is
frequently referred to, thus, e.g., at the world
conference of the International Council for Distance
Education in Melbourne in 1985. Examples of this
tendency are on the one hand the so-called contract
learning requiring of on-campus students study
independent of lectures and other face-to-face
teaching, on the other hand the growing use of
distance-study courses by on-campus students and the
application of information technology, which makes
it possible for students on and off campus to make
use of computer terminals and combinations of micro-
computing and telephone communication. In this way
the distinction between traditional education and
face-to-face communication may become blurred.

The use of ´distance` teaching on campus is
again nothing new, but known from the beginnings of
distance education, thus testifying to evolution
rather than revolution in distance education. The
´father` of American correspondence education,
William Harper, who died in 1906, introduced this in
Chicago. Bittner & Mallory 1933 report as follows:

> ...In addition to the service to off
> campus students, the Home Study Department
> is (1) continually assisting those on the
> campus, 1) by providing a means of
> completing residence courses necessarily
> dropped because of illness or calamity, 2)
> by enabling those whose obligations,
> financial or domestic, preclude attending
> certain prescribed or preferred courses,
> to get them at the proper time instead of
> waiting perhaps a year, 3) by accommo-
> dating those whose program would be
> disarranged because two desired courses
> come at the same hour, 4) by affording a
> means of repeating, along with a reduced
> residence program, in thoroughgoing
> fashion a course which in the first
> instance was not satisfactorily pursued`.

(Bittner & Mallory 1933, p.24)

The needs of distant students, necessarily or
voluntarily without recourse to face-to-face
teaching organisations for special study support
will remain, however. These needs will have to be
met by suitable methods, media, administrative
procedures and organisational patterns. Further
development of distance education in the sense

defined is thus to be foreseen at the same time as distance-teaching procedures are used in residential study.

We may have to think of gradations of distance in a literal and a figurative sense. Some students far away may wish to take part in study-centre activities, concentrated residential courses etc., and others within comfortable reach of the university, school or other type of supporting organisation may prefer entirely non-contiguous communication. It is difficult to imagine a future in which distance education will be de trop.

NOTES

1. This department was closed in 1964 (Mathieson 1971, p.2).

REFERENCES

Ashworth, K.H. (1978), The non-traditional
doctorate: time for sine cera? Phi Delta
Kappan, November 1978
Ashworth, K.H. (1979), Why I have not changed my
position. Phi Delta Kappan, April 1979
Ausubel, D.P. (1968), Educational psychology: A
cognitive view, New York, Holt, Rinehart &
Winston
Bååth, J.A. (1979), Correspondence education in the
light of a number of contemporary teaching
models, Malmo, LiberHermods
Bååth, J.A. (1980), Postal two-way communication in
in correspondence education, Lund, Gleerup
Bååth, J.A. (1981), On the nature of distance
education, Distance Education 2, 2, pp.212-219
Bååth, J.A. (1982), Distance students´ learning -
empirical findings and theoretical
deliberations, Distance Education, 3,1, pp.6-27
Bååth, J.A. (1984a), Pride and prejudice among
distance educators, ICDE Bulletin, 5, pp.70-73
Bååth, J.A. (1984b), Research on completion and
discontinuation in distance education, Epistol-
odidaktika, 1984, 1-2, pp.31-43
Bååth, J.A. (1984c), Essentials of distance educa-
tion (review of Holmberg 1982a), Teaching at a
Distance, 25, pp.120-122
Bååth, J.A. (1985), A note on the origin of distance
education, ICDE Bulletin, 7, pp.61-62
Bååth, J.A. & Månsson, N.O. (1977), CADE - a system
for computer-assisted distance education,
Malmo, Hermods
Bartels, J. & Hofmann, U. (1978), Analyse der
Studienabbrüche im Studienjahr 1976/77, Hagen,
FernUniversitat, ZFE
Bates, A.W. (ed.), (1984), The role of technology in
distance education, London, Croom Helm

REFERENCES

Battenberg, R.W., (1971), The Boston Gazette, March
    20, 1728, Epistolodidaktika, 1971:1, pp.44-45
Belchem, J. (1979), Teaching at a distance in
    Britain and New Zealand: some early
    impressions, Teaching at a Distance, 16, pp.2-6
van den Berg, B. (1984), Zur Entwicklung der
    Methoden des Fernunterrichts, dargestellt am
    Beispiel von Selbst- und Fernlehrmaterialien
    der Zeit von 1856 bis 1946, Dissertation,
    Aachen, Technische Hochschule, Pädag, Fakultat
Berte, N. (1976), Individualizing education through
    contract learning, Tuscaloosa, University of
    Alabama Press
Bittner, W.S. & Mallory, H.F. (1933), University
    teaching by mail, New York, MacMillan
Boucher, M. (1973), Spes in arduis - a history of
    the University of South Aftica, Pretoria,
    University of South Africa
Bratt, J. (1977), Engelskundervisningens framväxt i
    Sverige, Tiden fore 1850, Stockholm, Föreningen
    för svensk undervisningshistoria
Brezinka, W. (1976), Metatheorie der Erziehung,
    München, Reinhardt
Bruner, J. (1971), Toward a theory of instruction,
    Cambridge, Mass., The Belknap Press of Harvard
    University Press
Bückmann, N., Holmberg, B., Lehner, H. & Weingartz,
    M. (1985), ZIFF-Projekt 1-2.29: Fernstudien-
    systeme im internationalen Vergleich,
    Arbeitsfeld Lehren und Lernen, Steuerung
    und Selbständigkeit im Fernstudium,, Hagen
    FernUniversität, ZIFF
Burgess, T. (1972), The Open University, New Society
    27 April 1982
Carne, G. (1957), Hur H.S. Hermod började, Korres-
    pondens, 56, pp.44-45
Castro, A. & Holt, D. (1985), An introduction to the
    Open Campus Program at Deakin University, ICDE
    Bulletin, 9, pp.13-24
CEC Yearbook 1965, Leiden, CEC
CEC Yearbook 1966, Lincoln, CEC
CEC Yearbook 1967, Leiden, CEC
CEC Yearbook 1968, Copenhagen, CEC
Chamberlain, M. N. (1974), Courses by newspaper,
    ICCE Newsletter, 4, 3, pp.10-12
Chang, T.M., Crombag, H.F., van der Drift, K.D.J.M.
    & Moonen, J.M. (1983), Distance learning. On
    the design of an Open University, Boston,
    Kluwer-Nijhoff
Childs, G.B. (1963), Supervised correspondence
    instruction, The Brandenburg memorial essays on

correspondence instruction I, pp. 22-23 University of Wisconsin

Childs, G.B. (1965), Research in the correspondence instruction field, 7th ICCE Proceedings, pp.79-84, Stockholm, ICCE

Childs, G.B. (1971), Recent research developments in correspondence instruction. In MacKenzie, O. & Christensen, E.L. (eds.), The changing world of correspondence study, pp.229-249, University Park, Pennsylvania State University Press

Correspondence Instruction (1901), Unsigned article in Electrical Review, 14 December, 1901

Coughlan, R. (1980), The mentor role in individualized education at Empire State College, Distance Education, 1, 1, pp.1-12

Covill-Servo, J.L. & Hein, R. (1983), Towards a theory of instruction in the 1980s, Instructional Science, 12, 4, pp.301-319

Dahllöf, U. (1976), Reforming higher education and external studies in Sweden and Australia, Acta Universitatis Upsaliensis: Uppsala Studies in Education, Uppsala, Almqvist and Wiksell International

Daniel, J.S. & Marquis, C. (1979), Interaction and independence: getting the mixture right, Teaching at a Distance, 14, pp.29-44

Daniel, J.S., Stroud, M. & Thompson, J. (eds.), (1982), Learning at a distance. A world perspective, Edmonton, Athabasca University / ICDE

Daniel, J.S., Stroud, M. & Thompson, J. (1983), International Council for Distance Education, 1982 conference report and handbook, Edmonton, Athabasca University / ICDE

Delling, R.M.(1964), Gerhard Tersteegen und seine briefliche Seelsorge, Epistolodidaktika, 1964:1, pp.26-29

Delling, R. M. (1966), Der Einfluß der "Methode Rustin" auf das Fernunterrichts - und Fernstudien-Lehrmaterial der SBZ und der DDR, Epistolodidaktika, III:1, pp.18-24

Delling, R.M. (1971), Grundzüge einer Wissenschaft von Fernstudien, Epistolodidaktika, 1971:1, pp.14-20

Delling, R.M. (1975), Distant study as an opportunity for learning, in Ljoså, E. (ed.), The system of distance education, 1, pp. 58-59, Malmö, Hermods ICCE

Delling, R.M. (1978), Briefwechsel als Bestandteil und Vorläufer des Fernstudiums, ZIFF Papiere 19, Hagen, FernUniversität

REFERENCES

Delling, R.M. (1985a), Fernstudium in der Weimarer Republik, ZIFF Papiere 54, Hagen, FernUniversität

Delling, R.M. (1985b), Towards a theory of distance education, Paper read at the ICDE Conference in Melbourne, 13-20 August, 1985

Dinsdale, W.A. (1953), Inception and development of postal tuition, The Statist, 25 April 1953, pp. 572-575

Doerfert, F. (1980), Zur Wirksamkeit typografischer und grafischer Elemente in gedruckten Fernstudienmaterialien, (so far unpublished dissertation), Hagen, FernUniversität, ZIFF

Doerfert, F. (1984), Erste Ergebnisse zum Arbeitsfeld Medien, Zwischenbericht zum ZIFF-Forschungsprojekt Nr. 1.-2.29, Hagen, Fern-Universität, ZIFF

Dohmen, G. (1978), Das Zeitungskolleg als Lerngelegenheit, Fernkurse als Lerngelegenheiten. Texte des 3.BRIEF-Symposions über Fernstudium und Fernunterricht 1978, Tubingen, B.R.I.E.F. e.V.

Drake, M. (1979), The curse of the course teams, Teaching at a Distance, 16, pp.50-53

Einstein, A. & Infeld, L. (1950), Die Evolution der Physik, Hamburg, Zsolnay

El-Bushra, J. (1973), Correspondence teaching at university, Cambridge, International Extension College

Epistolodidaktika, (1963-), periodical published by Walter Schulz Verlag Hamburg, 1963-1970, and by the European Home Study Council, London, since 1971

Erdos, R. (1967), Teaching by correspondence, Unesco source book, London, Longman

Erdos, R. (ed.), (1969), Proceedings of the eighth international conference of the International Council on Correspondence Education, Paris, ICCE

Erdos, R. (1975), The system of distance education in terms of sub-systems and characteristic functions, in Ljoså, E. (ed.), The system of distance education, pp.9-19, ICCE, Malmö, Hermods

Evans, T.D. (1985), Just another brick in the wall: some reflections on student-based evaluation in distance education, Open Campus, pp.51-67, (Occasional papers published by the Distance Education Unit of Deakin University in Victoria, Australia)

Fales, A.W. & Burge, E.J. (1984), Self-direction by

149

design: self-directed learning in distance course design, Canadian Journal of University Continuing Education, X, 1, pp.68-78

Faure, E. et. al., (1972), Learning to be. The world of education today and tomorrow, Unesco, Paris, London, Harrap

Flinck, R. (1978), Correspondence education combined with systematic telephone tutoring, Kristianstad, Hermods

Fox, D. (1983), Personal theories of teaching, Studies in Higher Education, 7, 2, pp. 151-163

Från vision 90 till verklighet, (1985), Stockholm, Telematikskolan

Gaddén, G. (1973), Hermods 1898-1973, Malmö, Hermods

Gage, N.L. (1963), Handbook of research on teaching, Chicago, Rand McNally

General Circular, (1900), Scranton, Pa., The International Correspondence Schools

Glaser, B. & Strauss, A. (1977), The discovery of grounded theory, Chicago, Aldine

Göttert, R. (1983), Fernstudieninteressenten. Ihr Selbstbild und weiterer Studienverlauf, ZIFF Papiere 47, Hagen, FernUniversität

Graff, H. (1964), Die Briefe der Madame de Sévigné an ihre Tochter, Epistolodidaktika, 1, 2, pp.96-99

Graff, K. (1964), Briefwechsel und soziale Distanz, Versuch enuier soziologischen Theorie des belehrenden Briefes, Epistolodidaktika, 1, 1, pp.30-35

Graff K, & Holmberg, B. (eds.), (1984), Fernstudium im internationalen Vergleich-erste Ergebnisse, Hagen, FernUniversität, ZIFF

Granholm, G. (1971), Classroom teaching or home study - a summary of research on relative efficiency, Epistolodidaktika, 1971:2, pp.9-14, and 1973:2, pp.6-10

Green, B. (1979), Flexistudy - further education college-based distance learning with face-to-face tutorials, Aspects of Educational Technology XIII, Educational technology twenty years on, pp.94-96, London, Kogan Page

Groeben, B. (1972), Die Verständlichkeit von Unterrichtstexten. Dimensionen und Kriterien rezeptiver Lernstadien, Münster, Aschendorff

Hathaway, D.W. (1966), Advanced methods of using recordings, 7th ICCE Proceedings, pp.44-46, Stockholm, ICCE

Hawkridge, D.G. (1976), Setting up the Open University, Milton Keynes, The Open University

Hermod, H.S. (1908), Undervisning pr korrespondens,

Prospekt, Malmö, Malmö språk- & handelsinstitut

Holmberg, B. (1969), Educational technology and correspondence education, in Erdos, R. (ed.), Proceedings of the Eighth International Conference of the International Council for Correspondence Education, Paris, ICCE

Holmberg, B. (1973), Supervised correspondence study - a Swedish case study based on experiences within the school system, Epistolodidaktika 1973:2, pp.29-34

Holmberg, B. (1974), Distance education. A short handbook, Malmö, Hermods, (second, revised edition 1982)

Holmberg, B. (1976), Academic socialisation and distance study, Epistolodidaktika, 1976:1, pp.17-25

Holmberg, B. (1977a), Distance education. A survey and bibliography, London, Kogan Page

Holmberg, B. (1977b), Das Leitprogramm im Fernstudium, ZIFF Papiere 17, Hagen, FernUniversität

Holmberg, B. (1978), Fernstudiendidaktik als wissenschaftliches Fach, Hagen, FernUniversität, ZIFF

Holmberg, B. (1982a), Essentials of distance education, (a distance-teaching course, available also in a German version), Hagen, FernUniversität

Holmberg, B. (1982b), Recent research into distance education I-II, Hagen, FernUniversität, ZIFF

Holmberg, B. (1983a), Organisational models for course development, Epistolodidaktika, 1983:2, pp.14-27

Holmberg, B. (1983b), Establishing distance education as a university discipline - seven years of ZIFF research in Hagen, Higher Education in Europe, VIII, 3, pp.46-55

Holmberg, B. (1984), Professional development courses in distance education - a reply, Distance Education, 5, 2, pp.237-238

Holmberg, B. (1985a), Status and trends of distance education, second revised edition, Lund, Lector Publishing, Box 14010, S-22014 Lund, Sweden

Holmberg, B. (1985b), On the status of distance education in the world in the 1980s, - A preliminary report on the FernUniversität comparative study, Hagen, FernUniversität, ZIFF

Holmberg, B. & Schuemer, R. (1985), ZIFF-Projekt 1 - 2.29, Fernstudiensysteme im internationalen Vergleich, Erste Ergebnisse zum Arbeitsfeld: Beraten, Betreuen und Leistungskontrolle, Hagen, FernUniversität, ZIFF

REFERENCES

Holmberg, B., Schuemer, R. & Obermeier, A. (1982), Zur Effizienz des gelenkten didaktischen Gespräches, ZIFF Projekt 2.6, Schlussbericht mit einer englischen Zusammenfassung (with an English summary), Hagen, FernUniversität, ZIFF

Home Study, (1967-), periodical published by the National Extension College, Cambridge

Holt, D.M.(1985a), Theoretical models of evaluation, Open Campus, (occasional papers published by the Distance Education Unit of Deakin University in Victoria, Australia), pp.3-20

Holt, D.M. (1985b), Critical issues in evaluating learning material, Open Campus, (see preceding title), pp.21-50

Hosford, Ph.L. (1973), An instructional theory - a beginning, Englewood Cliffs, N.J.. Prentice Hall

ICDE Minutes, 1982, In Daniel, J.S., Stroud, M.A. & Thompson, J.R. (1983), pp.24-33, see above

James, B.J. & Wedemeyer, C.A. (1960), Completion of university correspondence courses by adults, The Home Study Review, 1, 2, pp.13-20

Jensen, G., Liveright, A.A. & Hallenbeck, W. (1964), Adult education. Outline of an emerging field of university study, Adult Education Association of USA (no place of origin stated)

Kaufman, D. (1982), Course development: industrial or social process, Paper presented at the American Educational Research Association, New York City

Kaufman, D. (1984), Practice and theory of distance education: course blue-print, Distance Education, 5, 2, pp.239-251

Kaye, A. & Rumble, G. (eds.), (1981), Distance teaching for higher and adult education, London, Croom Helm (in association with The Open University Press)

Keegan, D. (1980a), On defining distance education, Distance Education, 1, 1, pp.13-36

Keegan, D. (1980b), On the nature of distance education, ZIFF Papiere 33, Hagen, FernUniversität

Keegan, D. (1983), Six distance education theorists, Hagen, FernUniversität, ZIFF

Keegan, D. (1986), The foundations of distance education, London, Croom Helm

Klare, G.R. & Smart, K. (1973), Analysis of the readability level of selected USAFI instructional materials, Journal of Educational Research, 67, p.6.7

Korrespondens (1901-1975), periodical published by Hermods, Malmo, Sweden

Lampikoski, K. (1984), Boosts from computers in distance education, Epistolodidaktika,

1984:1-2, pp.58-73

Langer, J., Schulz von Thun, F. & Tausch, R. (1974), Verständlichkeit in Schule, Verwaltung, Politik und Wissenschaft, Munchen, Ernst Reinhardt Verlag

Lehner, H. (1978), Die Steuerung von Lernprozessen auf der Grundlage einer kognitiven Lerntheorie, Hagen, FernUniversität, ZIFF

Lehner, H. (1979), Erkenntnis durch Irrtum als Lehrmethode, Bochum, Kamp

Lehner, H. & Weingartz, M. (1985), Konfektionierung und Individualisierung im Fernstudium, Bericht zum ZIFF-Projekt 2.23, ZIFF Papiere 58, Hagen, FernUniversität

Leslie, J.D. (1979), Doing it differently at the University of Waterloo: courses by cassette, in Wentworth, R.B. (ed.), Correspondence education: dynamic and diversified, 2, pp.245-249, ICCE, London, Tuition House

Lessnoff, M. (1974), The structure of social science London, Allen & Unwin

Lewis, B.N. (1974), New methods of assessment and stronger methods of curriculum design, Milton Keynes, Open University, IET

Lewis, B.N. (1975), Conversational man, Teaching at a Distance, 2, pp.68-70

Light, H.R. (1956), Teaching by post, Talk given to Godalming Rotary Club 27 November, 1956, Mem. Croydon (?), Pitman Correspondence College

Lighty, W.H. (1915), Correspondence-study teaching, National University Extension Conference, Proceedings of the first conference, pp.75-83, Madison, Wisconsin, University of Wisconsin (?) reprinted in MacKenzie & Christenson (see below) pp.14-22

Ljoså, E. (1975), Why do we make commentary courses? in Ljoså, E. (ed.), The system of distance education, 1, pp.112-118, ICCE, Malmö, Hermods

Ljoså, E. (1977), Course design and media selection - some implications on co-operation between broadcasting, publishing and distance-education organizations, Epistolodidaktika, 1977:1, pp.75-84

Ljoså, E. & Sandvold, K.E. (1976), The student's freedom of choice within the didactical structure of a correspondence course, Paris, EHSC (also printed in Epistolodidaktika, 1983:1 pp.34-62, and in Sewart, Keegan & Holmberg (1983), pp.291-315 - see below)

Loser, F. & Terhart, E. (1977), Theorien des Lehrens Stuttgart, Klett

Macdonald-Ross, M. (1973), Behavioural objectives — a critical review, Instructional Science, 2, pp.1-52

Macdonald-Ross, M. (1979), Language in texts: a review of research relevant to the design of curricular materials, in Schulman, L.S. (Ed.), Review of Research in Education, 6, Itasca, Ill Peacock

MacKenzie, O. & Christensen, E.L. (Eds.) (1971), The changing world of correspondence study. International readings, University Park, Pennsylvania State University Press

Marshall, L. (1985?), Independence. Study contracts, second edition, Murdoch, W.A., Murdoch University

Marton, F. (1979), Learning as seen from the learners' point of view, ZIFF Papiere 30, Hagen, FernUniversität

Mathieson, D.E. (1971), Correspondence study: a summary review of the research and development literature, Syracuse, N.Y., National Home Study Council/ERIC Clearinghouse on adult education

McConnell, D. (1982), CYCLOPS telewriting tutorials, Teaching at a Distance, 22, pp.20-25

McIntosh, N., Calder, J. & Swift, B. (1976), A degree of difference, A study of the first year's intake to the Open University of the United Kingdom, Guildford, Society for Research into Higher Education

Methode Toussaint-Langenscheidt, Prospekt: zugleich Einleitung in den Unterricht (1901?), Berlin, Langenscheidt

Mohle, H. (1979), Distance education at universities and colleges in the GDR - the statutory foundation of its introduction and implementation, Leipzig, Karl Marx Universität

Mollers, P. (1981), Computergestutzte Lehre zum betrieblichen Rechnungswesen. Ein integriertes Modell, Hagen, FernUniversität, ZIFF

Moore, M. (1973), Towards a theory of independent learning, Journal of Higher Education, 44, pp.661-679

Moore, M. (1976), Investigation of the interaction between the cognitive style of field independence and attitudes to independent study among adult learners who use correspondence independent study and self-directed independent study, unpublished doctoral dissertation, Madison, University of Wisconsin

Moore, M. (1977a), A model of independent study, Epistolodidaktika, 1977:1, pp.6-40

REFERENCES

Moore, M. (1977b), On a theory of independent study, ZIFF Papiere 16, Hagen, FernUniversität

Moore, M. (1983), Self directed learning and distance education, ZIFF Papiere 48, Hagen, FernUniversität

Moore, M. (1985), Some observations on current research in distance education, to be published in Epistolodidaktika

Neuhoff, R. & Riechel, J. (1985), ZIFF-Forschungs-projekt 1-2,29: Fernstudium im internationalen Vergleich, Zwischenbericht zum Arbeitsfeld: "Organisation". Organisation von Fernstudien-systemen - Erste Ergebnisse, Hagen, Fern-Universität, ZIFF

Noffsinger, J.S. (1926), Correspondence schools, lyceums, chatauquas, New York, Macmillan

Open campus, Occasional papers published by the Distance Education Unit of Deakin University, Victoria, Australia

O'Shea, T. (1984), Computer-assisted learning in distance education, Epistolodidaktika, 1984: 1-2, pp.44-57

Parlett, M. & Hamilton, D. (1972), Evaluation as illumination: a new approach to the study of innovatory programs, Edinburgh: University of Edinburgh, Centre for Research in Educational Sciences

Pask, G. (1976), Conversational techniques in the study and practice of education, British Journal of Educational Psychology, 46, pp.12-25

Perraton, H. (1974), Is there a teacher in the system? Teaching at a Distance, 1, pp.55-60

Perraton, H. (1976), Two-way communication within a distance teaching system, in Granholm, G. (ed.), The system of distance education, 2, Malmo, Liber ICCE, pp.79-85

Perraton, H. (1978), I sat in H.G. Wells' chair, in Teaching at a Distance, 13, pp.1-4

Perraton, H. (1981), A theory for distance education, Prospects, XI, 1, pp.13-24, reprint-ed in Sewart, Keegan & Holmberg (1983) (see below), pp.34-45

Perry, W. (1970), Forms of intellectual and ethical development in the college years, New York, Holt, Rinehart & Winston

(Lord) Perry (W.) of Walton (1976), Open University, A personal account by the first Vice-Chancellor, Milton Keynes, The Open University

Peters, O. (1969), New perspectives in correspond-ence study in Europe, in Erdos, R. (ed.), Pro-ceedings of the eighth international conference

REFERENCES

of the International Council on Correspondence
Education, pp.94-105, Paris, ICCE
Peters, O. (1973), Die didaktische Struktur des
Fernunterrichts. Untersuchungen zu einer in-
dustrialisierten Form des Lehrens und Lernens,
Tübinger Beiträge zum Fernstudium 7, Weinheim,
Beltz
Peters, O. (1983), Distance teaching and industrial
production: a comparative interpretation in
outline, in Sewart, Keegan & Holmberg (1983),
(see below), pp.95-113
Popper, K. (1972), Naturgesetze und theoretische
Systeme, in Albert, H. (ed.), Theorie und Rea-
lität, Tubingen, Mohr
Popper, K. (1980), The logic of scientific discovery
London, Hutchinson
Potvin, D.J. (1976), An analysis of the andragogical
approach to the didactics of distance
education, in Granholm, G. (ed.), The system of
distance education, 2, pp.27-30, Malmö, Liber
Rayner, S.A. (1949), Correspondence education in
Australia and New Zealand, Melbourne, Melbourne
University Press
Rebel, K. (1984), Zur Konzeption der Arbeit des DIFF
in den achtziger Jahren - einige persönliche
Überlegungen, Tübingen:4 BRIEF-Symposion über
Fernunterricht und Fernstudium, unpublished
conference document
Reichmann, J. (1979), Die Zeitungskollegs, Fern-
studium aktuell, 1, p.5
Rekkedal, T. (1983), The written assignments in
correspondence education. Effects of reducing
turn-around time. An experimental study. (A
translation of Innsendingsoppgavene i
brevundervisningen of 1973), Distance Education
4, 2, pp.231-252
Rekkedal, T. (1985), Introducing the personal tutor/
counsellor in the system of distance education,
Project report 2: Final report, Oslo, NKI
Report of supervised correspondence study, (1934),
Summer school, Teachers College, Columbia
University, Scranton, P.A., ICS (?)
Rogers, C. (1969), Freedom to learn, Columbus,
Ohio, Merrill
Rogers, E.M. & Shoemaker, F.F. (1971), Communication
of innovation: a cross-cultural approach, New
York, The Free Press
Rothkopf, E.Z. (1970), The concept of mathemagenic
activities, Review of Educational Research, 40,
pp.325-336
Rumble, G. & Harry, K. (eds.), (1982), The distance

teaching universities, London, Croom Helm
Russel, B. (1951), An outline of philosophy, London, Allen & Unwin
Sacks, H. (1980), Flexistudy - an open learning system for further and adult education, British Journal of Educational Technology, 11, 2, pp.85-95
Sewart, D. (1978), Continuity of concern for students in a system of learning at a distance, ZIFF Papiere 22, Hagen, FernUniversität
Sewart, D. (1981), Distance teaching: a contradiction in terms? Teaching at a Distance, 19, pp.8-18, reprinted in Sewart, Keegan & Holmberg (1983), (see below), pp.46-61
Sewart, D., Keegan, D. & Holmberg, B. (eds.), (1983) Distance education. International perspectives, Beckenham/Kent, Croom Helm
Sheath, H.C. (1969), External studies at university level - some recent developments, 8th ICCE Proceedings, pp.117-139, Paris, ICCE
Simon, H.A. (1973), Does scientific discovery have a logic? Philosophy of Science, 40, pp.471-480
Sims, R.S. (1977), An inquiry into correspondence education processes: Policies, principles and practices in correspondence education systems worldwide, (unpublished ICCE-Unesco report)
Smith, K.C. (1975), External studies at the University of New England. An exercise in integration, in Ljoså, E. (ed.), The system of distance education, 1, pp.161-169, Malmo, Hermods ICCE
Smith, K.C. (1979), External studies at New England, Armidale, NSW, The University of New England
Smith, K.C. (1983), Putting the student first: some personal perspectives or a tale of two serpents, in Daniel, J.S., Stroud, M.A. & Thompson, J.R. (eds.), International Council for Distance Education. 1982 conference report and handbook, pp.12-21, Edmonton, Athabasca University/ICDE
Smith, K.C. (ed.), (1984), Diversity down under, Toowoomba, Darling Downs Institute Press
Snow, R.E. (1973), Theory construction for research on teaching, in Travers, R.M.W. (ed.), Second handbook of research on teaching, Chicago, Rand McNally
Sommer, K.H. (1965), Der Fernunterricht, seine Wirklichkeit und Problematik unter besonderer Berücksichtigung des berufsbezogenen "Briefunterrichts" in der Bundesrepublik Deutschland, Laasphe, Adalbert Carl

Stewart, D. (1976), Higher Education courses through newspapers, _Epistolodidaktika_, 1976:2, pp.60-73

Store, E. & Chick, J. (1984), Reaching out in Queensland: a decentralised approach, in Smith, K. (ed.), _Diversity down under_, Toowoomba, Darling Downs Institute Press

Taylor, P.C. (1985), Illuminating primary distance education in Australia, _Programmed Learning & Educational Technology_, 22, 4, pp.320-326, London, Kogan Page

Taylor, P. & Tomlinson, D. (1985), _Primary distance education. Population, problems and prospects_, Nedlands, National Centre for Research on Rural Education

The Home Study Review, periodical published by the National Home Study Council, Washington, D.C.

The International Correspondence Schools. How to proceed with your studies, (1898, 1899), Scranton, Pa., The Collicey Engineer Company

Thomas, L.F. & Harri-Augstein, E. S. (1977), Learning to learn: the personal construction and exchange of meaning, in Howe, M.J.A. (ed.), _Adult learning. Psychological research and applications_, London, Wiley

Thorpe, M. (1979a), When is a course not a course? _Teaching at a Distance_, 16, pp.13-18

Thorpe, M. (1979b), The student special support scheme: a report, _Teaching at a Distance_, 15, pp.1-14

Tomlinson, D., Coulter, F. & Peacock, J. (1985), _Teaching and learning at home: distance education and the isolated child_, Nedlands, The University of Western Australia

Valkyser, H. (1981), _Fernstudiensystemkonforme Beratung und Betreuung als didaktische Elemente einer Zweiweg-Kommunikation im Fernstudium – unter besonderer Berücksichtigung bisheriger Erfahrungen an der FernUniversität_, Hagen, FernUniversitat, (Diss.)

Vincent, A.T. (1982), Computer-assisted support for blind students – the use of a micro-computer linked voice synthesizer, _Computers & Education_, 6, 11, pp.55-60

Vincent, G.E. (1900), Going to college by mail, _Sunday School Times_, (USA), 1 July, 1900

Vincent, J.H. (1886), _Chatauqua movement_, Boston, Chatauqua Press

Vonk, H.G. & Brown, R. G. (1978), The external doctorate in education: growing criticism and crisis, _Phi Delta Kappan_, November 1978

Wagenschein, M. (1975), _Verstehen lehren_, Weinheim, Beltz

REFERENCES

Waller, R.(1977a) Three functions of text presenta-
    tion, Notes on Transforming 2, Milton Keynes,
    The Open University, IET
Waller, R. (1977b), Typographic access structures
    for educational texts, Milton Keynes, The Open
    University, IET
Wedemeyer, C.A. (1981), Learning at the back door,
    Reflections on non-traditional learning in the
    lifespan, Madison, University of Wisconsin
Weingartz, M. (1980), Didaktische Merkmale selbstin-
    struierender Studientexte, Hagen, FernUniversi-
    tät, ZIFF
Weingartz, M. (1981), Lernen mit Texten, Bochum,
    Kamp
Weinstock, N. (1975), Les cours par correspondance
    du secteur privé en Belgique, Bruxelles. Centre
    National de Sociologie du Droit Social
Weissbrot, E. (1969), Specific aspects of supervised
    correspondence study with school children, 8th
    ICCE Proceedings, pp.163-177, Paris, ICCE
Weltner, K. (1977), Die Unterstützung autonomen
    Lernens im Fernstudium durch integrierende
    Leitprogramme, ZIFF Papiere 17, pp.2-14, Hagen,
    FernUniversitat
Willmott, G. & King, B. (1984), Professional
    development courses in distance education,
    Distance Education, 5, 1, pp.116-130
Wolsey Hall, Oxford. Prospectus of correspondence
    courses and external students' guide to London
    University examinations (1914), Oxford, The
    Omega Press
Woolfe, R. (1974), Social equality as an Open
    University objective, Teaching at a Distance,
    1, pp.41-44
Worth, V. (1982), Empire State College/State
    University of New York Center for Distance
    Learning, DERG Papers 7, Milton Keynes, The
    Open University
Zimmer, R.S. (1981), The relational glossary: A
    tool for effective distance learning, in
    Percival, F. & Ellington, H. (eds.), Aspects of
    Educational Technology, XV, Distance learning
    and evaluation, pp.73-79, London, Kogan Page

INDEX